7·19·79

HOPE FOR HEALING

HOPE FOR HEALING

An invitation to Hope and Healing
through personal and social relationships.

BY GEORGE LEACH

PAULIST PRESS
New York, N.Y./Ramsey, N.J.

PAULIST PRESS
Published by arrangements
with Daniel Books of Toronto
ISBN 0-8091-2178-6
Library of Congress
Catalog Card Number 78-70231

Published by Paulist Press
Editorial Office 1865 Broadway, New York, N.Y. 10023
Business Office 545 Island Road, Ramsey, N.J. 07446

ILLUSTRATION–NANCY PERRY
DESIGN–VIRGINIA MORIN & NANCY PERRY

PHOTOS–LEO CAMERON, O.S.A.; DAS STUDIOS, DARJEEL-
ING, INDIA; JEAN GORECKI, JOHN LYON; DONNA MOYSEUIK;
YOUTH CORPS, TORONTO.

ACKNOWLEDGEMENTS
Many friends have assisted me in creating this book. Its early
beginnings stirred in different L'Arche communities throughout the
world. It grew through dialogue with my Jesuit brothers in Canada
and India. The Faith & Sharing groups, which celebrate their 10th
anniversary this summer, inspired me in countless ways. So many
people supported and encouraged me that it would take pages to
name them.

But, some I must single out. Mary Kay urged the actual work
when she transcribed the original tapes. Pat encouraged the writing,
as Lynn was typing the first draft. At a point of hesitation Sue
introduced me to Dan. His careful eye, keen suggestions and gentle
patience enabled me to continue, indeed to finish. Mike read
carefully the final manuscript, which Sabrina had typed and retyped
with quiet dedication. Finally, Nancy and Ginny did the layout and
design. Their creativity and enthusiasm thrilled me. For all the
support and encouragement of these many, many friends, and
above all for their love, I am deeply grateful.

CONTENTS

2058014

For my mother – healer,
　　　healing,
　　　　　hopeful on earth

　　and

my father – healed,
　　　healing,
　　　　　held in eternity.

This short book has sprung from the heart of a priest of Jesus. Before being a book, these words were a message, a message of faith, a message of hope and a message of love. They were shared during a Faith and Sharing retreat in Saskatoon and they became the seeds of the Spirit, sown in the hearts of those who listened. The words of this little book are not just to be read but are to be seen as a vehicle of a presence, the presence of the Invisible, Gentle, Wounded, and Risen Healer.

Father George is a precious friend, a brother in Jesus. We are walking together as His disciples. The words of Father George have always brought me peace and joy, the presence of God; they are healing words, bringing us the presence of the Healer.

I pray and hope that all those who receive the gift of this book will find the liberation that the Healer has promised us. He reveals and takes away from our being our darkness and sinfulness and then in our weakness calls us forth to become healers of all men and women, our brothers and sisters, particularly the most wounded.

Jean Vanier

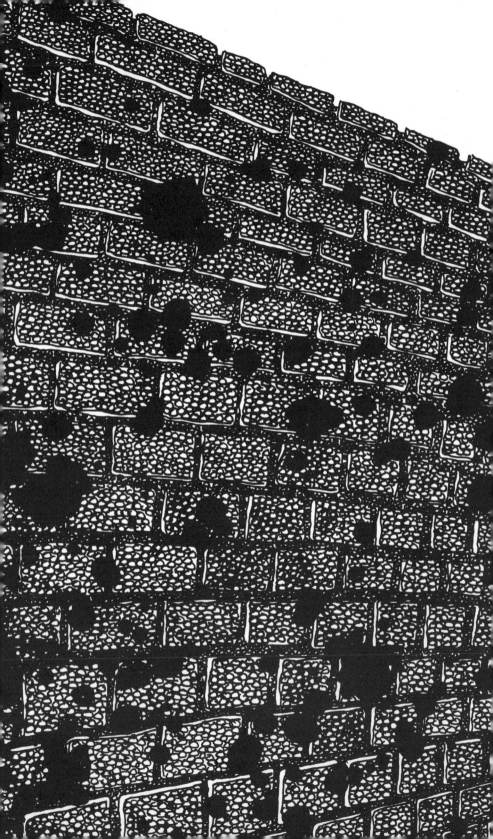

Introduction

Healing presupposes pain. Some kind of disorder emerges in man. From a common cold to terminal cancer, we have a huge continuum of pain. A plethora of human suffering crowds our world. The TV brings world hunger into our living rooms. The newspapers remind us of countless violent deaths in accidents and wars. Reports of racial strife in South Africa call for justice. Continued bloodshed between Catholics and Protestants keeps Ireland in turmoil. The imprisonment of missionaries and the lack of religious freedom in South America and other countries shock our sensitivities. The economic crises, the political stance in many countries, the number of foreign investments, all speak of power and possible pain. The international scene ripples with pain. How will we ever meet this?

In our own backyard, we have strife between brothers and sisters, between the sexes, between black and white, between native and non-native peoples. We have seething wounds around biculturalism, bilingualism, separatism. A piercing pain often appears revealing racist bias and contempt. Age old misunderstandings, bad experiences, outright prejudice fester and eat away at nations, at people, causing sores and pains that seem sometimes almost insurmountable.

The plight of the Native Peoples of North America floods the media from time to time. The settlement of landclaims is crucial. A fair return for timber cutting and terrain changed through development projects calls for better negotiations. The danger of obliterating a culture, indeed a people, looms like a foreboding, dark raincloud. Respect for men and women who see the land as their life invites all North Americans to mutual respect. These realities call for our attention. Deep pain rests in many. Justice is one route to healing but we will need a deep love and mutual trust in each other. Will we dare to enter a relationship? Will we dare to love?

Maybe the Red man, the White man, the Black man or the Yellow man is not part of my experience. Maybe I don't think I'm racist. I doubt it. Yes, each of us lives with certain biases and prejudices. A little reflection will quickly reveal a garden of weeds. How do I feel

3

about the Pakistanis? the Jews? the drunks? the bums? the skid row men and women? "I'm not like them," do we sigh. Or, do we self-righteously say, "There but for the grace of God go I." So much racism, disorder, sinfulness rumble around in us. What kind of healing do we need? How will this come about? Who will make us whole?

What is happening in family life these days? If we believed everything that appears in the public press, the future looks dismal. Divorce and separation pour down like a monsoon. Infidelity is like an ever flooding river. Many people ponder whether marriage is possible. The young flounder when they see the floods of non-commitment. Inter-family strife sends adolescents running. Where? – to dope; to booze; to sex. The pain is excruciating in so many. Is there any hope for healing?

Single people often seem to be stalking the streets in isolation. The lonely crowd, the gang of isolated individuals, even couples on a date who talk at, not with each other, all reveal the wrenching pain of loneliness. The apartment dwellers cut themselves off at the 15th storey behind locked doors. The aged peer from behind wise eyes having no one with whom to share. The alcoholic, drunk again, stumbles in his latest stupor. The prostitute, male or female, sells his/her body. Where is the relationship? Is love possible? What do we fear? What are we running from?

Or, we can look at the people in our institutions. Our hospitals are becoming more crowded and less staffed. What does this say of the patient care? The stress among nurses, doctors and support-staff grows. How do they handle financial cut-backs and rotating shift work, to mention only two problems. How will we meet the tension of our penal institutions? Hostages, the "hole" (solitary confinement), and sexual aberrations, all shock the outsider. Prison reform is a must. Or, a mental patient escapes. The papers panic. Fear floods the heart of man, but what will he do? What does one say to an unwanted child, to a single parent, to a divorcee? What can we do for, or might we dare suggest, how can we live with the "labelled" person? "He's handicapped, retarded, strange," they say. But, what do *we* say? What crosses our mind when we read about the labor disputes? high school teachers on strike? the uprisings that caused the Kent State University explosions a few years back, the Brampton High School slayings in southern Ontario? – and there are more, many more.

So much personal suffering and hidden pain exist around us, indeed in many of us. If we dare to look in the mirror, pause and reflect, we might break the mirror and run. Does irritation ever lead us to frustration, even anger and hostility? A simple comment can shift our mood. A glance can even change our feelings. Maybe fear lurks in the recesses of our being. What will trigger the emotional content that frightens us, scares us, unleashes fear? Maybe domination and control pervade our life. We need to have everything just so. Or, more subtly, we control others by our compliments. Manipulation is another manifestation. However we cut it, pride is rampant. Healing is necessary. Maybe one of the deepest and most crippling pains is self-pity. The "poor-me" attitude squeaks out of so many. People feel so sorry for themselves that they can be emotional paralytics, lost in their own world; they spiral into isolation and become grossly unattractive to others. They despair, as they are tossed on their sea of hopelessness. Their very problem compounds their problem. Our world needs so much healing. Our country needs so much healing. We need so much healing. And it begins with us. Where then, and how, will we begin?

Two people who have met the challenge to be healers in our day are Mother Teresa and Jean Vanier. Mother Teresa of Calcutta stepped out of her comfortable cloister to care for the dying. She has moved to the poorest of the poor, men and women who have nothing. From the street people of Calcutta, New York and Lima to the aborigines of Australia, her love permeates this oft forgotten world of pain. When a few of us were chatting with her one day in Calcutta, we inquired how we might help her from Canada. In utter simplicity she said: "Love your brother" These words ring often in my ears.

Jean Vanier is my friend. From my first visit to L'Arche, (the Ark) in Trosly-Breuil, France, through the many short but profound encounters with Jean over the past seven years, I grow in gratitude for our friendship. When Jean first said: "If you open your heart to the handicapped, you can open your heart to anyone," I knew the Spirit was sparking this man. I met him some three or four years after he had founded his first community with the mentally handicapped. I have shared deeply with him as the Canadian L'Arches have sprung into being. Jean is a man of boundless energy, tender love and peaceful prayer.

But we are not Jean Vanier or Mother Teresa. We are not founders of communities for the dying or the handicapped. Our call is not theirs. But we, too, have a call. The Spirit sparks each of us with good desires. Despite our pain, our suffering, our confusion, moments of love, peace, hope emerge. Amidst a personal malaise, desires for the good surface. What a mixture we are! Weeds and flowers grow simultaneously in the garden of our hearts. Who will tend this garden? Who will hoe, spade and water? Who will give the increase?

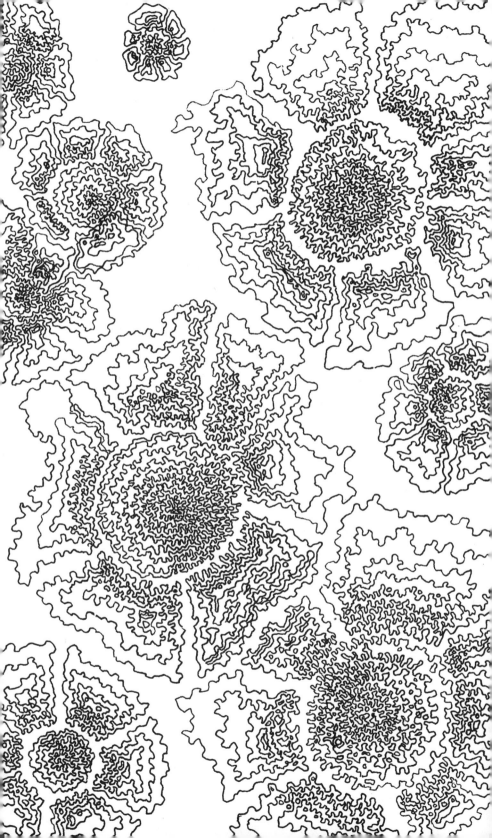

THE INVITING HEALER

Healers have been present
A quick glance through history reveals different healers. Men have stood for others in firing squads. Prisons have held the innocent, sometimes by their own choice. Mothers have died that children might live. National leaders have been assassinated for the cause of justice and freedom. The spirit of helping, the urge to heal, rests in the heart of MAN.

Man has hoped in man
Down the ages of time individuals have reached out and touched the deeper HUMAN SPIRIT. Amidst wars and famines, cyclones and catastrophes, people have emerged as signs of hope. From concentration camps to mental asylums, from prisons to hospitals, the human person has transcended suffering. Meaning has come. Healing has happened. Hope has been present.

The creation of a family rises instinctually in us. Its extention to grandparents, aunts and uncles, friends and neighbors, broadens and deepens the concentric circles of love. Today, families young and old, people married and single, group together with a desire to serve others. Men and women dedicated to God and their fellow human beings are living together in the hope of an alternate life style. New forms of the extended family and other unique living patterns are appearing on the human horizon. People are recognizing the need for meaningful, profound and lasting relationships. The orientation of our lives is interpersonal. As men and women, we are social beings.

The call is a simple one: build the human family...

          provide an occasion for mankind to
          grow, to expand...

          invite the people of God to flower
          and flourish...

          create a place where love is,
          will be...

          a situation where healing can
          take place.

This is our invitation!

What is our response?

Do we have the urge to heal,
the spirit to help?
          or, do we hurt too much ourselves
            to see and hear others?

Does the pain of injustice
      and
        the lack of freedom
                pervade the fibers
                  of our being?

What about others whose pain
         and
         aches
              are constantly
               before us?

What can we do?

        Where can we turn?

              To whom can we go?

For 2000 years God's living word, Jesus Christ, has opened vistas of possible healings.

Jesus Himself said: "I have come so that they may have life and have it to the full." *(John 10:10)* He invites us to live. Now is the time to grow in this fullness, a time to meet others and ourselves in Christ. Jesus speaks to us from his own personal experience, through his encounters with people, his personal sufferings and death. Redemption came through His sufferings. His death invites us to a more meaningful life. His resurrection, moreover, is the basis of all Christian life.

Jesus is the center of Christian living

Jesus is the center of all Christian experience. If anything profound is to happen to us, it will be in relationship with Jesus Christ. We will meet Him. We will encounter Him in some way. We will look into His eyes; hear His words; see His works; love Him. We will let our hearts be open to the possibility that His spirit can move in our hearts. We will allow our minds to be moulded by His spirit. We will be open to the reality of *metanoia*, change and conversion.

We sometimes strikingly see this relationship with Christ, this encounter with His Person. We may meet Him along the way, when we meet a handicapped person. Christ's spirit has overflowed into their lives and, in turn, touches into our lives. Once a person experiences love and acceptance, he or she reciprocates with growing love and acceptance.

For example, Gary who lives at Caritas House, a L'Arche Home near Stratford, Ontario, loves and accepts each new visitor as a long, lost friend. His ready smile and quick 'hello' welcomes everyone. His warm handshake and friendly chatter underlines the welcome. His bounce and vitality engenders warmth immediately. Although the conversation may be dis-jointed, with confused genders or in-correct time sequences, his face, eyes and hands all communicate his love. His heart is on his sleeve. His feelings overflow. He is present. He loves.

His unique openness and presence to people more than makes up for his mental lack. In fact, he has a richness that many people might envy. When you hear Gary tell people that he likes them, or he tells you, it makes you feel good. Most people smile. How good it is for our hearts to hear that we are loved! How healing it is to be told that we are loved! How good to know that someone cares!...and yet, we have so many inhibitions and hesitations about caring for others and expressing our concern. What a freedom many handicapped people have! What a call to us! What a grace they are!

Gary's intriguing personality can open us to others. People down the street, our neighbor next door, within the family or community, human persons can engage us. Indeed, people who are different catch our eye, make us think, ponder and wonder.

If we read the Bible, we see Jesus meeting people, talking to them, healing them, urging them and inviting them. He moves in varying relationships. People respond to Him in different ways.

John the Baptist's encounter with Jesus evolved. At first the people thought John was Jesus. But, when asked 'Who are you?' he said in the words of Isaiah, the prophet: "a voice that cries in the wilderness. Make a straight path for the Lord." *(Isaiah 40:3)* When challenged why he was baptizing, if he was not the Christ, he replied:

"I baptize with water, but there stands among you –
unknown to you – the one who is coming after me and I
am not fit to undo his sandal strap." *(John 1:26-27)*

John knew he was not the Christ. He awaited Christ. He pondered and preached; he raised and answered questions. John can become a meaningful person for us if we find ourselves in some way like him. When we come to that moment in our lives, when we pose similar questions: 'Who are you? why am I alive? what is meaningful?' or the like, we know we have found a kindred spirit in John.

Some people are plagued with questions and doubt. Others claim to know nothing. They retire from the mystery of life. They are the walking dead. But, to question, to doubt, to wonder is deeply human. To probe the mysteries of creation captivates the scientist, the philospher, the theologian. Man is born to ask 'why', to seek knowledge and to love. This is human nature.

'Who is this man, Jesus?' is not a surprising question. Related questions in faith and philosophy are normal. Since Jesus is the God-Man, the Word-Incarnate, questions and doubt must arise. This challenges the thinking human person.

Jesus is the central mystery of the Christian faith. His very life, His questions, His way of living, He Himself lead the human person to question, to probe, to seek understanding. If a person really believes in Jesus and the Christian faith, he will have questions. "Who is this man Jesus? I want to know Who He is. I want to come to a deeper knowledge of Him, a stronger love for Him."

In Matthew's Gospel Jesus asked his disciples: "Who do men say that I am?" *(Matthew 16:14)* Remember Peter's answer: "You are the Christ, the Son of the living God." *(Matthew 16:16)* It is important to note how Peter came to this. We find out from the words of Jesus. "Simon, son of Jonah, you are a happy man! Because it was not flesh and blood that revealed this to you, but my father in heaven." *(Matthew 16:17)* Don't we live like Peter and John with our questions, doubts, ponderings, and hopes? Indeed, John, Gary and Peter can be meaningful persons for us. They can bring us Christ. How else will we meet Him?

As life unfolds in an everyday experience or at special times of enlightenment or prayer, the invitation is the same – share and grow in faith-life-love. Meet Christ. The call comes to care for an aging relative, to participate in an issue of social justice, to visit a prison. They are all cut from the same fabric, the fabric of loving service.

But the radical invitation in our busy, buzzing culture is to find some quiet time. To still the pumping heart and quiet the surging pysche might be symbolized by the escalator. Have you ever found yourself running up the up-escalator? Why? To save 5 seconds! But, to stand still on the escalator and watch people run in the stores and subways can be a moment of stillness and calm. To seize moments for tranquillity and calmness even amidst the hustle and bustle of life can quiet us. At what pace do we want to run? jog? walk? How fast is the inner person moving? What do we really desire?

This radical invitation to find some quiet time is essential to soothe the spirit. We need to slow down, to listen to ourselves, to creation and our God. Take time to walk alone in the park or down a country lane. Listen to your heart. Still your mind by letting your thoughts drift away like a flock of birds from a tree. Listen to the sounds of nature. Birds. Dogs. Trees. Let God speak to your still, silent heart. Treasure these moments. Go silently before the seemingly silent Lord. Let Him tell you Who He is. Let Him touch your heart. Let Him mould your mind. Let Him build a personal relationship.

There are many ways that we can learn of the Lord. We can begin as John the Baptist or St. Peter did. We can learn from Gary or another friend. We can catch a fleeting moment on a busy day or step aside for an hour, a day, maybe even a week-end to be still, silent and in solitude. We give Jesus the opportunity to heal. We begin or continue the process of becoming more human, more Christian. We are evolving. This Christic evolution brings us to be witnesses like John the Baptist, St. Peter and Gary.

> The next day, seeing Jesus coming towards him, John said, 'Look, there is the lamb of God that takes away the sin of the world. This is the one I spoke of when I said: a man is coming after me who ranks before me because he existed before me. I did not know him myself and yet, it was to reveal him to Israel that I came baptizing with water . . . Yes, I have seen and I am the witness that he is the Chosen One of God.'   (John 1:29-34)

The invitation is that we see; we too need the eyes of John the Baptist. We need the heart to discover the person, Jesus, in Himself and in His people. We ask for that disposition. We seek openness to the Holy Spirit. We want to recognize His 'resting' on people, His 'living' in people. We pray for a clarity like John's, a sureness like Peter's and an openness like Gary's. We desire to know Jesus more clearly, to love Him more dearly and to follow Him more nearly.

To help this knowledge and love grow we look more deeply into the relationship between John the Baptist and Jesus.

> On the following day, as John stood there again with two of his disciples, Jesus passed, and John stared hard at him and said, 'Look there is the Lamb of God.' Hearing this, the two disciples followed Jesus. Jesus turned round, saw them following and said, 'What do you want?' They answered, 'Rabbi', which means Master, 'Where do you live?' 'Come and see', he replied. So, they went and saw where he lived and stayed with him the rest of that day.
>
>   (John 1:35-39)

LOOK, THERE IS THE LAMB OF GOD!

The Scripture points us to Jesus!

Do we hear His question?

WHAT DO YOU WANT?

Do we have their question?

WHERE DO YOU LIVE?

Do we hear His response?

COME AND SEE!

Gary,
my friend,
Where do you come from?

      your blue eyes...deep, hurting, dancing,
                         sometimes gaunt.
      your lean body...quick, surging, agile,
                         some days bent.
      your gait, your glance, your touch,
         all speak...no, scream of wounds wrapped
                                 round
                                 and
                                 round
                         a tender heart.

Gary,
my friend,
who has moulded you?

      your call came as unexpected as Jeremiah's;
      your conversion kept you up all night, scurrying
                with Christ;
      your vocation causes pain to you, and to others;
      your friendship thrills me, your brother.

Gary,
my friend,
where will you go?

> ripped from a new rooting...rootless? No!
> freed from an old haunting...never! Yes?
> frayed by paining memories...maybe? maybe!
> loved by so very many...Yes! Yes! Yes!

Gary,
my friend,

> I know where you come from.
> I love Him Who has moulded you.
> I serve with you, wherever you go,

>> because, we are one,
>> companions of the One,
>> friends of the Friend,

>> and

>> brothers of our Brother.

>> I love you.

Jesus invites but never forces. He beckons, holds out His hand and waits freely. He does not give an address. Where He lives is not a place. He lives in the present. He lives in the Kingdom, His Kingdom. He does not have a specific country with a special language. His Kingdom is the Kingdom of the heart. He will teach his disciples about this new life. He will give them the beatitudes and enflesh them. He will teach them about the gifts of the Holy Spirit by living them. He will call them to be strong but tender, firm but gentle, compassionate and kind, by loving them. He will teach them about healing by healing. He will predict His Passion and prophesy His Resurrection. His is a school of life through death and resurrection after suffering. His message is hope; His meaning his love.

His disciples went and saw. Perhaps this is our invitation today. Will He live in our hearts? Will we enter His Kingdom? Do we hear His question?

WHAT DO YOU WANT?

Some pondering, some reflection, some still-time could unearth what we want. Are we really in touch with our deepest desires? Money? Intelligence? Possessions? Peace? Friendship? Love? Children? Jesus? How do we cut through the bombardment of TV advertisement to find out what we want and desire? Has our culture totally formed our desires? Does the media tell us what we want? Have we settled into a stupor of passivity? What activates our deeper human spirit? What stimulates an active response? What engages men and women in creative life?

When Jesus asks, "What do you want?", if we are really going to listen, He will speak. We may hear different possibilities, be led in different ways, reach a different goal, but the Spirit of Jesus will be with us. He will create and re-create us in His Kingdom. He will form us into the family of mankind, build us into His Body, the Church – a new community of love.

This call is not without its struggle. John the Baptist pointed to Christ, actually baptized him at the Jordan, witnessed to Him in Judea but with time ended up in prison. St. Matthew explains:

Now John in his prison had heard what Christ was doing

and he sent his disciples to ask him, "Are you the one who is to come, or have we got to wait for someone else?" Jesus answered, "Go back and tell John what you hear and see; the blind see again and the lame walk, lepers are cleansed and the deaf hear, the dead are raised to life and the good news is proclaimed to the poor; and happy is the man who does not lose faith in me." *(Matthew 11:2-6)*
The pain of prison, its loneliness, questions, doubts converge to cause John some self-doubt. Is He really the Christ? Is my life real? Is it worth it? Did I make a mistake? Honest, sincere questions! Sometimes we have the same turmoil.

GO BACK AND TELL HIM WHAT YOU SEE.

Jesus did not answer him directly and say, "Yes, I am the Christ!" Rather, He tells the disciples to go back and tell him what they see. They go and share their faith with John. They tell him about the poor, the deaf and the blind. They tell him what they see and hear. They share their new life with him. But Jesus then confronts the crowds.

WHAT DID YOU GO OUT INTO THE WILDERNESS TO SEE?

As the messengers were leaving, Jesus began to talk to the people about John. "What did you go out into the wilderness to see? A reed swaying in the breeze? No? Then, what did you go out to see? A man wearing fine clothes? Oh no, those who wear fine clothes are to be found in palaces. Then, what did you go out for? To see a prophet? Yes, I tell you, and much more than a prophet. He is the one whom the Scripture says: "Look, I am going to send my messenger before you; He will prepare your way before you." *(Matthew 11:7-10)*

John is that man, born to say: "make the path straight...prepare yourselves...repent...Christ, the Lamb of God, is coming!" Listen to the love Jesus has for John.

I tell you solemnly, of all the children born of women, a greater than John the Baptist has never been seen; yet the least in the kingdom of heaven is greater than he is. Since John the Baptist came, up to this present time, the kingdom of heaven has been subjected to violence and the violent are taking it by storm. Because it was towards John that all the prophecies of the prophets and of the law were leading, and he, if you will believe me, is the Elijah who was to return. If anyone has ears to hear, let him listen.   *(Matthew 11:1-15)*

Then, of course, the strong invitation to John, and to us, is to believe, to trust and have faith. The message comes back to John via the disciples: "The blind see, the deaf hear, the lame walk, the poor have the good news proclaimed to them." What message comes to us? to our country, our culture? How will we experience this good news?

Les pauvres, the *Anawhim,* the casualties of our culture are the weak and poor around us. In fact, most of us are not strong and powerful, the rich. But we do have many gifts, talents and riches, both in material possessions and personality. For the most part, we are in the middle class. When we honestly look at our lives, we see the world from our middle class perspective. Sometimes, this appears as a personal prison. We find ourselves barred in, locked in on ourselves. We deeply desire freedom. Our riches have shackled us, bound us. We need someone to come, open the door of our cell and say: 'come, come and see'. We need to get out of our prison so we can love. Whether we are lower or middle class poor, whether we are the poor suffering among the very rich – isolated, alcoholic or whatever, the invitation is the same – freedom to love. This opportunity arises because Jesus has issued the initial call to human freedom and love. He wants us, peaceful and non-violent, forgiven and free, to respond to Him. He wants us out of our prison, freed from the bars of ourselves. He desires us to come and see, to open our minds and hearts, to listen and relate to Him, to prepare His way, to live His new life.

Whether it is John the Baptist and Jesus, or Peter and Jesus, or you and I, it is a relationship. If we read and reflect on the passages about John the Baptist, we can see the relationship. At the Jordan River he said: "That's the Lamb of God, the Anointed One, the one who will go to the slaughter." John knew Jesus. They had a relationship. From his prison cell John suffered, doubted and questioned in the relationship. He knew he had to believe and trust; he had to let the relationship grow and develop with its ups and downs, ins and outs. Their relationship was real, human and interpersonal, as it unfolded and expanded.

Isn't this a model for our relationships? Don't John and Jesus teach us? Don't we find ourselves here? What do we do?

THERE ARE MANY WAYS TO PRAY

The person, Jesus, how do I relate to Him? What do I say to Him? What is He saying to me? To what is He calling me? How does He want me to pray?

There are many ways to pray. Prayer can be as simple as a friend of mine calling it – 'the dialogue of the double look' – 'He looks at me and I look at Him; we don't talk much, but we communicate a whole lot.' We sit quietly without many words. We are just there. A prayer of presence. At other times, our prayer is vocal. We read or recite mentally from a book or memory. The mind is active, posing questions and pondering responses. We meditate. Then again, our prayer can be more imaginative with images, words and actions, flowing from the Scriptures. We see the scene, listen to the words and perceive the action of the text. By recalling the event, we allow the good-news of Jesus to touch our time. We contemplate. In these moments of silence His Spirit can permeate our hearts.

But the form our prayer takes really doesn't matter. What matters is the relationship. The 'mattering' is . . . I am being drawn into love, because I am being drawn to God. And **GOD IS LOVE**. *(1 John 4:8)*

The beautiful base of my relating to God is the fact that God is relational. The Father relates to Jesus, His Son, and this begets the Holy Spirit. Their loving relationship overflows to the marvelous creation of our world and all mankind. This triune love saved all men and women through the life, death and resurrection of Jesus Christ, the Second Person of the Trinity. Today, their loving relationship continues redemption calling every human person to conversion, commitment and union with Them.

ONE POSSIBLE RESULT OF PRAYER IS HEALING

Did you ever see someone in love about to be married? You chat with them, look into their eyes, and what do you see? Someone in love is different. They have changed. They are caught up in someone outside themselves. The other is more important. They live for them. They are quieter, more humble and much more gentle. A loving relationship has a deep and profound effect.

In the Gospels Jesus related to many people. He went up and touched some. He related physically by touch when he put clay and spittle on the blind man's eyes. He took people by the hand. He let the children come to Him.

But how does He heal our hearts? How do we change? How do we hear the Lord through the prophet Ezechiel: "I shall remove the heart of stone from your bodies and give you a heart of flesh instead." *(Ezechiel 36:26)* How will He heal us?

One possible result of prayer is healing, but all healing is going to be relational. The kind of healing we immediately think of is physical. Healing is also emotional, psychological and spiritual. Jesus forgave sins, calmed His flustered friends and of course, cured the physically sick. For us, then, to be healed, in whatever way we need, we must enter a relationship with Jesus Christ. We dare to enter this mode of loving, opening ourselves to the possibility of becoming more and more like Him. To move in this way with Jesus, to live like Him, will mean that my love will overflow to others.

As we enter the sounds of silence, praying to God, seeking to be like Christ, begging for the Spirit of Love, we will quickly find out that our relationship to the Trinity is not all pure and white. There are shades of gray, and sometimes, if not often, we discover our inability to love. We see that we are weak, self-centered, sinful. At other times, we are open and responsive with desires to love and serve. Sometimes, we just hope and long for a deepening of the relationship. We want to grow in Christ. We desire healing, freedom and love.

The supportive surprise is that Jesus wants all this more than we can imagine. He spent His life calling people to love. He gave His life to prove His love. "A man can have no greater love than to lay down his life for his friends." *(John 15:13)*

The challenge is to respond to His invitation.

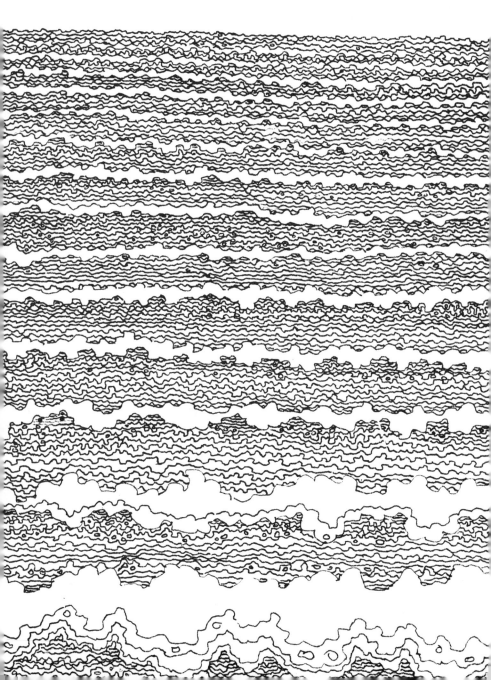

A hand reaches to a hand...
                    creating.
A heart suffers for a heart...
                    redeeming.
A spirit surges for a spirit...
                    celebrating.
A presence desires a presence...
                        union.

My hand reaches to Your hand...
                        co-creating.
My heart suffers for Your heart...
                        co-redeeming.
My spirit surges for Your spirit...
                        concelebrating.
My presence desires Your presence...
                        communion.

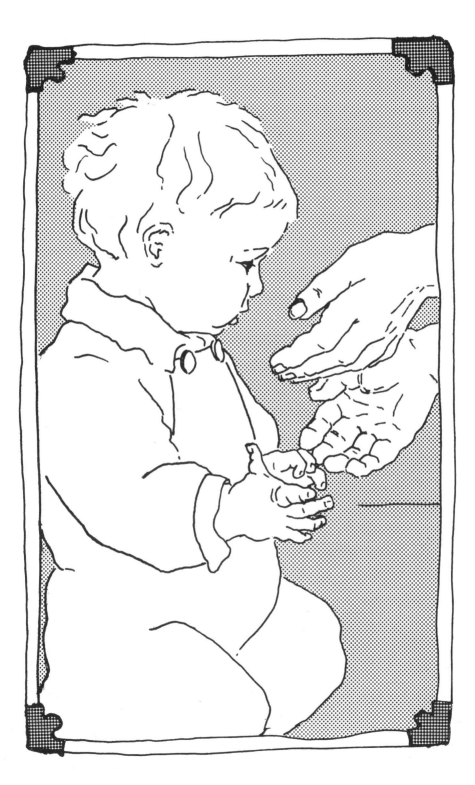

Enter the mystery of silence . . . go to the solitude of
your private room . . . find the silence of a still spot in creation,
and say . . .

WHO ARE YOU?

WHERE DO YOU LIVE?

HOW TO YOU WANT ME TO LIVE?

WHAT ARE YOU CALLING ME TO?

WHY AM I ALIVE?

(now, pause. . .be still, listen, wait. . .be silent)

What is my prison?   What are my bars?
        my violence?   my walls? (for walling in
        my sin?   and walling out)
                        my blocks?
                        my barriers?

(now, pause...be still, listen, wait...be silent)

How am I to love?
            relate?

                        believe?
                        trust?

                                                hope?
                                                pray?

(now pause...be still, listen, wait...be silent)

HURTING...HELPING...HOLDING...HEALING...
                                by JESUS
                                by me.

PRAYING...PLEADING...PLEASING...by Jesus
                                by me.

read... reflect... ponder...

The Father calls...

> The word of Yahweh was addressed to me, saying,
>   'Before I formed you in the womb I knew you...
> I said, 'Ah, Lord Yahweh; look, I do not know how to speak:
>   I am a child!'
> But Yahweh replied, 'Do not say, "I am a child".
> Go now to those to whom I send you
> and say whatever I command you.
> Do not be afraid of them,
> for I am with you to protect you...
>
>   *(Jeremiah 1:4-8)*

> Then I heard the voice of the Lord Saying:
>   'Whom shall I send? Who will be our messenger?'
> I answered, 'Here I am, send me'.
>
>   *(Isaiah 6:8-9)*

Jesus invites...

When Jesus came to the region of Caesarea Philippi he put this question to his disciples, 'Who do people say the Son of Man is?' And they said, 'Some say he is John the Baptist, some Elijah, and others Jeremiah or one of the prophets'. 'But you,' he said 'who do you say I am?' Then Simon Peter spoke up, 'You are the Christ,' he said 'the Son of the living God'. Jesus replied, 'Simon son of Jonah, you are a happy man! Because it was not flesh and blood that revealed this to you but my Father in heaven.

(Matthew 16:13-18)

As he was walking along by the Sea of Galilee he saw Simon and his brother Andrew casting a net in the lake – for they were fishermen. And Jesus said to them, 'Follow me and I will make you into fishers of men'. And at once they left their nets and followed him.

(Mark 1:16-18)

The Spirit urges...

He went in and said to her, 'Rejoice, so highly favoured! The Lord is with you.' She was deeply disturbed by these words and asked herself what this greeting could mean, but the angel said to her, 'Mary, do not be afraid; you have won God's favour. Listen! You are to conceive and bear a son, and you must name him Jesus. Mary said to the angel, 'But how can this come about, since I am a virgin?' 'The Holy Spirit will come upon you' the angel answered 'and the power of the Most High will cover you with its shadow. And so the child will be holy and will be called Son of God.'   (Luke 1:28-32, 34-36)

Suddenly, while he was travelling to Damascus and just before he reached the city, there came a light from heaven all around him. He fell to the ground, and then he heard a voice saying, 'Saul, Saul, why are you persecuting me?' 'Who are you, Lord?' he asked, and the voice answered, 'I am Jesus, and you are persecuting me. Get up now and go into the city, and you will be told what you have to do.' The men travelling with Saul stood there speechless, for though they heard the voice they could see no one. Saul got up from the ground, but even with his eyes wide open he could see nothing at all, and they had to lead him into Damascus by the hand. For three days he was without his sight, and took neither food nor drink.   (Acts 9:3-9)

respond... review... peace...

THE GENTLE HEALER

The Man Who Loves
Jesus, the gentle healer, the Man who loves, shows forth His healing in many forms. That He desires to have a strong, deep, personal relationship with each one of us is clear from His public life. His desire is pain, if you want, the pain of love. His life proves it; His life invites us. And the heart of any real healing is the heart of Christ.

Freedom to Love
From time to time, from within our own hearts, emerges a deep personal desire to love. At times we wonder whether to enter the mystery of love or back away. We all know we are deeply a mixture. We experience this with our friends in different ways. We are ambivalent creatures. Our road might be long and wide, but as we strain for that freedom to love, we yearn to give deeply. We desire to be richly human and long to live more fully. Our hope and prayer is that each person will grow in that *freedom to love,* in that communion of our heart and His heart.

Freedom to Discover
To assist this growth in freedom to love, we take time to think, to reflect. We come to pray. To ponder freely, to think peacefully, to pray quietly can mean assuming different bodily positions. The important thing about the freedom of body positions is that I dispose my body to listen, to hear the inner spirit, the revealed Word. So, whether I sit or stand, stroll or kneel, it really does not matter. The important awareness is to have the *freedom to discover* how we can be present to the inner and the Other. Some people kneel; they are at

peace...they pray. Other people stand; a quietness takes over...they ponder. Some people like to prostrate themselves. Some assume the lotus position before the Lord. In Christian prayer, the important aspect is that I am before the Lord. My body is disposed to be there in peace, in stillness and tranquility. This is the freedom of spirit that says it does not matter how we pray, thank, adore and ask the Lord. The important reality is the adoration, thanksgiving, praise and petition.

The invitation is to move into the 'sounds of silence'. Some prompting moves us into the music of a relationship so the Spirit can draw us to know, love, serve, get excited about, cry over, and maybe even weep for Jesus Christ. The invitation is to solitude, to peace, to sharing, to take time to be still. As He creates us in freedom and calls us to love, we will relax and be. The suggestion is to open the Scriptures, to read a bit and mull over the meaning. What is happening in the passage? What are the people saying? What are they doing? What do we see as we imagine the scene? Let it speak. If you come to a part that is alive for you, stay with it. Just remain in union with the Lord and let Him do the work.

...relax...imagine...respond...

In North America we are very work orientated. In our culture we say, "we are going to do it." Well, prayer is the reverse. In prayer all we do is dispose ourselves. It's like having our hands open and relaxed, not closed or grabbing. We dispose our minds and hearts to be like a sponge, ready to receive water to the full. The more we 'let go' in prayer, the more we let the Lord move and work, the more possibilities for change emerge. We can be healed by His Spirit. We can grow and integrate our personalities. It is like the parable of the sower:

> As he sowed, some seeds fell on the edge of the path and the birds came and ate them up. Others fell on patches of rock where they found little soil and sprang up straight

away because there was no depth of earth; but as soon as the sun came up they were scorched and, not having any roots, they withered away. Others fell among thorns, and the thorns grew up and choked them. Others fell on rich soil and produced their crop, some a hundredfold, some sixty, some thirty. *(Matthew 13:4-9)*

The seed has been sown. We are the garden in which that word of God has been planted. He wants to grow; He wants to come forth and produce fruit. He desires to heal whatever needs to be healed. He wants to stir our faith, activate our love and create us in hope. He desires to bring us to Himself as we live and serve among men and women. As He says through the Prophet Hosea; "I was like someone who lifts an infant close against his cheek; stooping down to him I gave him his food." *(Hosea 11:4b)* How gentle! Have you ever watched a mother do that to her baby? That is the kind of gentle healing that the Father has for each of us.

Our culture, on the other hand, says to be tough, hard, strong. Do not show any gentleness. But, gentleness is not softness; it's not wishy-washy or mamby-pamby. It's love – a gentle love that is firm and strong, but tender. It's the gentleness of a father holding firmly the hand of his young daughter. This is the gentleness each of us desires.

Jesus was very gentle. One of the marvelous passages in which His gentleness comes forth is His encounter with the woman at the well in the Samaritan town. John, the Evangelist, describes it.

Jacob's well is there and Jesus, tired by the journey, sat straight down by the well. It was about the sixth hour. When a Samaritan woman came to draw water, Jesus said to her, "Give me a drink." His disciples had gone into the town to buy food. The Samaritan woman said to him, "What? You are a Jew and you ask me, a Samaritan, for a drink?" Jews, in fact, do not associate with Samaritans. Jesus replied: "If you only knew what God is offering and who it is that is saying to you: Give me a drink, you would have been one to ask, and he would have given you living water." *(John 4:5-11)*

He was tired; He was thirsty and asked for a drink of water. He was hungry and the disciples had gone to town to get some food.

Jesus was a man like you and me!
>He ate and drank;
>He grew tired and slept;
>He laughed and cried;
>He pained. . .

>>and prayed.

>He lost. . .

>>and loved.

Jesus was a man with the same needs as you and me. We are reminded in the New Testament:

>It is not as if we had a high priest who was incapable of feeling our weaknesses with us, but we have one who has been tempted in every way that we are, though He is without sin. *(Hebrews 4:15)*

He was there at the well. He began to enter into a human relationship with the woman when

>He said: "give me a drink of water," and

>she replied: "what are you talking to me, a Samaritan, for?"

>>In some places, we might think or even say:

>>"You shouldn't talk to me, I'm black. . .

>>>Jewish. . .

>>>Indian. . ."

>With whom do we enter relationships?
>Whom do we avoid?
>>How do we meet people?
>>>What color is love?

I remember . . . a field
brown and yellow,
and a man came to plow.

I remember . . . the field
furrowed and fallow,
as the man sowed his seed.

I remember . . . the corn
sprouting and reaching,
as the crop grew and grew.

I remember . . . the stalks
higher and higher,
as green life surged skyward.

I remember . . . the growth
stock by stock,
like an army lined to march.

I remember . . .

I remember . . . my field
brown and yellow,
and a Man came to plow.

I remember . . . my field
furrowed and fallow,
as the Man sowed His seed.

I remember . . . my life
sprouting and reaching,
as my love grew and grew.

I remember . . . the steps
little by little,
as new life surged upward.

I remember . . . the growth
step by step,
like a child-pilgrim-plodding.

I remember . . .

One morning, when I was in India, I arose and went to the well to get water to shave. I met a woman drawing water. You can imagine what went through my mind. She was a Bengali lady and I could not speak her language. Likewise, she knew no English. But an interesting thing happened. As I went to draw water, she took my bucket and filled it. In India, the women draw the water. I stepped back nervously as she drew the water. The next day I went back and thought, "I'm going to fill my own bucket." I filled mine and hers at the same time. She was surprised. It was a whole shift, a cultural change. "You shouldn't let a man, let alone a white man, fill your bucket!" probably surged in her mind. I was white and big, compared to this Indian lady. But gradually we became friends, without words. She began to realize that it was a very cultural thing, a different custom. And so did I. Whether she filled the bucket or I did, really didn't matter. But the relationship did. Friendship ensued.

When Jesus asked the woman at the well to give Him a drink of water, He was moving gently into a relationship with someone with whom He should not be speaking. He was transcending culture and custom. God may call and invite us into relationships with people whom we least expect. We may even find ourselves among the culturally unacceptable of our country. A teenager lives with the handicapped. What will the parents say? A Sister serving in a prison might shock some. What is she wasting her time there for? Or, the person who is faithful to the chronic alcoholic. Why bother? Maybe we are called to something like that. Do we tend to step aside? Do we put people away, out of sight, because, if out of sight, then out of mind! Often, we do not want to be reminded to what Jesus calls us.

The relationship to the Samaritan woman is more than hunger for food and drink as we all know. For Jesus replies:

> If you only knew what God is offering and who it is that is saying to you: Give me a drink, you would have been the one to ask, and he would have given you living water.
>
> (John 4:6-10)

At this point she does not know who this man is. Puzzled she queries:

> You have no bucket and the well is deep, how could you get this living water? Are you a greater man than our father Jacob who gave us this well and drank from it

himself with his sons and his cattle?

Jesus replied:

> Whoever drinks this water will get thirsty again; but
> anyone who drinks the water that I shall give will never be
> thirsty again; the water that I shall give will turn into a
> spring inside him, welling up to eternal life. *(John 4:11-14)*

When we come to times of reflection, days in the desert, or moments of prayer, we come with an empty cup. He will fill our cup from the bucket of living water. He has to give the living water. We dispose ourselves; we wait patiently before God; we listen; we hear . . . but, He must come with the Spirit. It is His gift to give. It is a welling up to eternal life. When He gives us a taste of the living water, our thirst is deepened for more living water. When the Spirit of God moves, when we have tasted His peace and gentleness, we want more. His quenching increases our thirsting!

Our hearts are sometimes hardened and sometimes, it's like water striking a rock. It splashes off and does not get into the soil of our hearts. Like the woman we ask, "How are you going to do this? You don't even have a bucket!" We pull back because we are not sure.

"Give me some of that water so that I may never get thirsty and never have to come here again to draw water." *(Jn. 4:15)* Something is happening. She is beginning to see that there is more to this encounter. Jesus is inviting her to something very different, a spiritual relationship. How gently He will now show her something very deep and very personal, but it could be very painful. He says to her: "Go and call your husband and come back here." *(John 4:16)* to her reply, "I have no husband," Jesus says:

> You are right to say, 'I have no husband', for although
> you have had five, the one you have now is not your
> husband. You spoke the truth there. *(John 4:18-19)*

Can you imagine what would happen if someone began to unfold that to us, started to help us see ourselves. He did not do it in a condemnatory way. He stayed very present to her and said: 'this is the way you are.' He did not even tell her to return to her first husband. Their relationship moves along peacefully and gently. But it is truth. She is not hiding. She is not pretending there is no sin, no disorder. He is saying, 'this is truth.' But He is loving her so much that she responds and says:

I see you are a prophet sir. Our fathers worshipped on this mountain, while you say that Jerusalem is the place where one ought to worship. *(Jn. 4:19-21)*

Jesus goes on to talk about worshipping in spirit and truth. Whether it be in Jerusalem or Jericho, in New York or Montreal, it does not matter. We worship God. He will call the woman into that relationship, into the relationship of the Kingdom. He so delicately reveals the truth to her about herself. This is self-revelation and self-knowledge. When Jesus does that, He does it very gently. He does not do it negatively. He comes in truth, and she, or we, admit, 'yes, I have sinned; yes, there is this side of me, this part of me that needs healing; and needs it very deeply. This is the healing that sets us free. This is the living water that makes us even more thirsty for Him.

Christ reveals us to ourselves if we will let Him. Sometimes we do not like this self-revelation. The incredible reality is that He loves us exactly as we are; we do not have to be anybody else. There is only one Mother Teresa, only one Jean Vanier. The beautiful thing is that God loves each of us uniquely. Juliana's strength from her wheelchair could never be compared to Larry's insight through his blindness. Jesus gives each of us the desire, the yearning, the grace to be and to become. To accept this and say, "this is who I am," requires His gift. "I do not have to be someone I am not. I do not even have to try. Who wants to be that other person anyway? He has given me myself. I am the one He wants. He loves me!" So Jesus calls us to a very truthful relationship and we realize very quickly that He is our God and we are His people. He has longed for us from the moment of creation.

We are created in His image, to be like Him – the God of Love, the God of Freedom. We are born to be with Him, to live our lives in union with Him. We blend the human and the divine when we unite with Him in moments of truth. The ultimate moment of truth is death, the moment of deepest freedom. We enter eternal life.

Jean Vanier once said: "We should live in relationship with people so that when you're not there, you're missed, and someone will cry at your funeral." How do we form these kinds of relationships? How do we become keenly attentive to each other? How do we become really present? How do we relate so that it makes a difference?

Wherever we are, and with whomever we live, we will be present at many levels and in different ways. We may simply grunt a 'good morning' over coffee. We may open the day in a silent reflection, alone or with some others. We may burst from our beds rested and refreshed. Work can be a complete bore or an interesting challenge. People can be a problem or a graced moment. The car, the bus, the subway can all be a drag or an invitation. What we do with our time, our day, our life, will all open a myriad of possibilities. How deeply and in what way will we relate?

Jesus was so present to the woman at the well that He could perceive her need. Then He moved in ever so gently. She was being drawn, converted, changed, until finally she ran to town to tell everybody, "Come and see a man who has told me everything I ever did; I wonder if he is the Christ?" (Jn. 4:29) She has been set free by the truth. Her freedom overflows in an enthusiastic response. She goes to spread the Good News, to tell her friends about Jesus. Don't we know something about Him too? What is He really offering to us?

This woman at the well in Samaria was obviously loved, and she knew it. When we are loved, we do all kinds of things. It is amazing what the power of love can do. When we are loved and when we love, one of the strongest effects is that we become gentle. Unsolicited love disarms; it just 'blows your mind'. Love that one does not expect. . . surprising love. . . you did not know someone cared. What a gift!

Let us hope that the Spirit will move in us. Let us seek to see what Jesus said and did. Let us focus on a freedom to live and love. He invites us to be like Him. "Come follow Me!" It is as simple and profound as washing dishes, changing a tire, fixing a step or preparing a meal. These are simple incarnations of love. This is loving service. What an extraordinary call!

Jesus calls us into a relationship of gentleness. Have you ever had the experience where you are a little edgy and someone speaks very gently to you? To speak softly can heal hurt. It often melts the eruption.

Have you ever been present when an argument explodes? A heated exhange, verbal blows, fierce looks go back and forth. Do we step into the fray or mentally step back? Can we stay present and not fan the fire of anger?

What will we do?

To return gentleness for violence will gradually expel it,
                                        eradicate it.

To listen beyond the words,
            below the argumentation can still us and
                            have us ponder . . .

        "I wonder what the real pain is?"
        "How can I come gently like Jesus into this person's life?"

To wait patiently until the venom is all out is sometimes the only
            way to care,
                to be present,
                to really heal.

We wait . . . we listen . . . we love.

   We need the gentleness of Jesus deeply within us before we can
ever meet the pain in others or in ourselves. If our own hearts are
healed and gentleness runs deep, then we can meet suffering,
wherever it is.
   Each of us has weakness from which we run. Each of us has love
which we hesitate to share. Each of us needs to receive. Each of us
needs the growth of gentleness, the fact of reconciliation. We are at
times fragile, needing support; at other times weak, needing
strength; sometimes we feel alone, needing companionship; at times
we are isolated, needing a community; or sinful, needing grace; fearful, needing love. How important this is! How we need gentle,
peaceful people for our personal healing, indeed for all healing.

Let us pause now for some quiet time.
Let us go before God to discover in the sounds of silence.

Discover the gentle movement that is going
on inside us all the time.
Discover the many ways of loving and
receiving love.
Discover the many ways that Jesus,
the gentle healer, is trying to love in us.
Discover His call to a freedom,
a healing that will
allow us to love. . .
a healing that will
call us to be gentle healers with Him,
like Him,

Be still.
Be.

Thank You for creation,
for the darting sun
splitting the clouds and
caresssing the lake.

Thank You for creation,
for the tumbling waterfall
spilling over rocks and
rushing to the lake.

Thank You for creation,
for flitting snow
falling through the trees and
melting on my face.

Thank You, my Creator,
for Your Gentle Self
softening my hardness and
loving my ingratitude.

Thank You, My Lord
for Your Gentle Son,
speaking of love and
inviting to love.

Thank You, my Father,
for Your Gentle Spirit
teaching me freedom and
freeing my spirit.

JESUS HEALS...

imagine...picture...ponder...

The woman who was a sinner
    One of the Pharisees invited him to a meal. When he ar-
rived at the Pharisee's house and took his place at table, a
woman came in, who had a bad name in the town. She
had heard he was dining with the Pharisee and had
brought with her an alabaster jar of ointment. She waited
behind him at his feet, weeping, and her tears fell on his
feet, and she wiped them away with her hair; then she
covered his feet with kisses and anointed them with the
ointment.
    When the Pharisee who had invited him saw this, he
said to himself, 'If this man were a prophet, he would
know who this woman is that is touching him and what a
bad name she has'. Then Jesus took him up and said,
'Simon, I have something to say to you'. 'Speak, Master'
was the reply. 'There was once a creditor who had two
men in his debt; one owed him five hundred denarii, the

other fifty. They were unable to pay, so he pardoned them both. Which of them will love him more?' 'The one who was pardoned more, I suppose' answered Simon. Jesus said, 'You are right'.

Then he turned to the woman. 'Simon,' he said 'you see this woman? I came into your house, and you poured no water over my feet, but she has poured out her tears over my feet and wiped them away with her hair. You gave me no kiss, but she has been covering my feet with kisses ever since I came in. You did not anoint my head with oil, but she has anointed my feet with ointment. For this reason I tell you that her sins, her many sins, must have been forgiven her, or she would not have shown such great love. It is the man who is forgiven little who shows little love.' Then he said to her, 'Your sins are forgiven'. Those who were with him at table began to say to themselves, 'Who is this man, that he even forgives sins?' But he said to the woman, 'Your faith has saved you; go in peace'.

(Luke 7:36-50)

The Pharisee and the Publican

He spoke the following parable to some people who prided themselves on being virtuous and despised everyone else, 'Two men went up to the Temple to pray, one a Pharisee, the other a tax collector. The Pharisee stood there and said this prayer to himself, "I thank you, God, that I am not grasping, unjust, adulterous like the rest of mankind, and particularly that I am not like this tax collector here. I fast twice a week; I pay tithes on all I get." The tax collector stood some distance away, not daring even to raise his eyes to heaven; but he beat his breast and said, "God, be merciful to me, a sinner". This man, I tell you, went home again at rights with God; the other did not. For everyone who exalts himself will be humbled, but the man who humbles himself will be exalted.'

(Luke 18:9-14)

Cure of a paralytic

Now he was teaching one day, and among the audience there were Pharisees and doctors of the Law who had come from every village in Galilee, from Judaea and from Jerusalem. And the Power of the Lord was behind his works of healing. Then some men appeared, carrying on a bed a paralysed man whom they were trying to bring in and lay down in front of him. But as the crowd made it impossible to find a way of getting him in, they went up on to the flat roof and lowered him and his stretcher down through the tiles into the middle of the gathering, in front of Jesus. Seeing their faith he said, 'My friend, your sins are forgiven you'. The scribes and the Pharisees began to think this over. 'Who is this man talking blasphemy? Who can forgive sins but God alone?' But Jesus, aware of their thoughts, made them this reply, 'What are these thoughts you have in your hearts? Which of these is easier: to say, "Your sins are forgiven you" or to say, "Get up and walk"? But to prove to you that the Son of Man has authority on earth to forgive sins,' – he said to the paralysed man – 'I order you: get up, and pick up your stretcher and go home.' And immediately before their very eyes he got up, picked up what he had been lying on and went home praising God.

They were all astounded and praised God, and were filled with awe, saying, 'We have seen strange things today'.   *(Luke 5:17-26)*

reflect... review...

pray.

THE
COMPASSIONATE HEALER

Jesus, our true friend, invites us into a deeper relationship with Him. We have seen Him healing others through His gentleness. Let us explore another aspect of healing that happens in a relationship – compassion.

When a compassionate person crosses our path, there is something about him or her that relaxes us. In his presence we begin to feel change, to experience interior movement, to feel more real, more whole. He loves us with our weakness, handicap, suffering. We sense a total acceptance.

The compassionate person usually says very little. Their great capacity is to listen, to be present. In a way, they take on our sufferings.

Many times a compassionate person has suffered deeply, but often not by choice. No one likes to suffer. Even Jesus did not want to suffer. At Gethsemane He said to the Father; "Everything is possible for you. Take this cup away from me. But let it be as you, not as I, would have it." *(Mark 14:36)* However, this was the way to redeem the world. He was ready to go to His passion to become the Man of Compassion.

If we look around our world, we see pain on many horizons. Each day we see suffering in the newspapers and on television, but after awhile what does it really mean? What does the hunger in the Third World really do to us? How do we react to a drought or famine in Africa, to the exploitation of people by large multi-national companies in countries of South America? What do we think about the new economic order? The issues are endless.

'I can't rush off to Africa and drill for water, or go to Calcutta and distribute food to the poor!' This thought has probably surfaced in our minds. Maybe we have even felt guilty. Even though most of us cannot do this, each of us can ask ourselves in the reality of our own country 'To what am I being called? How will I build the human family here? How will I serve? How will I become a man or woman of compassion?'

"You have the poor with you always." *(John 12:8)* Jesus also taught: "How happy are you who are poor, yours is the kingdom of God." *(Luke 6:20)* Our call is to open our hearts to the world, especially to the poor. In opening our hearts to those around us, to those in our family, our community, our parish, in school or at work, then our hearts will be open to all men.

Jean Vanier said that 'if you can open your heart to the handicapped, you can open your heart to anyone.' Sometimes it takes a friend like Giles whose crippled body speaks pain but whose enlivened spirit draws us to really open ourselves. Sometimes another person frightens us. We withdraw. We close ourselves because we become fearful of their personal presence. We hesitate. Or, we may meet someone who is confused, upset, disturbed in some way. No matter what the situation, if we open our heart to the person, usually we will receive. At times there is pain to be received; and who really wants to receive pain? At other times, there is joy to experience. We expand and grow. Whatever comes, we hope to stand free to become men and women of openness, joy and compassion.

The heart of Christ is compassionate. His own words are:

Be compassionate as your Father is compassionate. Do not judge and you will not be judged yourselves; do not condemn and you will not be condemned yourselves; grant pardon and you will be pardoned. Give and there will be gifts for you: a full measure, pressed down, shaken together and running over, will be poured into your lap; because the amount you measure out is the amount you will be given back.   *(Luke 6:36-38)*

To understand the caring of Jesus, to understand how much he desires to be with us, to suffer with us, to take on our pain, is to know the compassionate healer.

In the parables He really reveals the mercy and the love of His Father. You remember the story of the lost Drachma.

What woman with ten drachmas would not, if she lost

one, light a lamp and sweep out the house and search thoroughly till she found it? And then, when she had found it, call together her friends and neighbors? 'Rejoice with me,' she would say, 'I have found the drachma I lost.'

(Luke 15:8-10)

When the woman found the money, there was great rejoicing. One of the new biblical translations talks about a dime and one wonders how we could rejoice in finding a dime. AMONG THE DESTITUTE POOR, A DIME IS REALLY SOMETHING. In India, if one could get two and one-half rupees (a dollar equals about 8 rupees) a day, he could get enough rice for one meal. A poor man must work all day to get two and one-half rupees. If he has a dime, at least he can buy something, even if it is only a small amount. When one lives as the poorest of the poor, with no security or conveniences that we know in North America, one lives day to day, moment to moment. To live with the hope that maybe today we'll forage for and find food, one can see why some would rejoice in finding a dime. Even a responsible relationship to money, however small, creates people of concern.

What man among you with a hundred sheep, losing one, would not leave the ninety-nine in the wilderness and go after the missing one till he found it? And when he found it, would he not joyfully take it on his shoulders and then, when he got home, call together his friends and neighbors? 'Rejoice with me,' he would say, 'I have found my sheep that was lost.' In the same way, I tell you, there will be more rejoicing in heaven over one repentant sinner than over ninety-nine virtuous men who have no need of repentance. *(Luke 15:4-7)*

Using images, Jesus tries to show and convey to the people His Father's compassion. Imagine...the shepherd had ninety-nine sheep and he is concerned about one little sheep who gets lost in the woods. What incredible concern! He is going to spend his time looking and searching. This is the compassionate love of our God.

To move from object (drachma), to animal (sheep), to people we have the parable of the Prodigal Son. *(Luke 15:11-32)* We all know the story well. We have read it, thought about it, and probably said: "That's me!" "I'm the prodigal son!" If we read a little deeper, we may realize..."I'm the older brother too!"

This parable reveals the heart of the Father. He saw his son coming back. He was looking. He was not sitting dis-interestedly by the fire. I wonder how often he went out and looked to see if his son was coming up the road.

> While he was still a long way off, his father saw him and was moved with pity. He ran to the boy clasped him in his arms and kissed him tenderly.   *(Luke 15:20-21)*

Anyone who has children who have been lost knows what it is like. It's supper time and Freddie is not home. Where is he? You go and look for him – backyard, frontyard, neighbor's house, playground – where is he? You have not seen him all day! It happens – you feel the anxiety rising and you wonder . . . will he return? Is he lost? Has he drowned? been killed?

THE LONGING FOR A LOVED ONE...

YOU MISS YOUR HUSBAND
              WHO TRAVELS FOR HIS BUSINESS FIRM.
YOUR WIFE IS AWAY WITH THE CHILDREN ON VACATION.

SOMEONE YOU CARE FOR, LONG TO SEE, IS SEPARATED
              BY MANY MILES.

SEPARATION CAN CAUSE SUFFERING.
WITH REFLECTION AND PRAYER IT CAN BECOME

              COMPASSION.

The father ran to meet his son when he saw him coming; he clasped him and kissed him tenderly. The strong, strong affection that he had. The joy he experienced.

> "Quick! Bring out the best robe and put it on him; put a ring on his finger and sandals on his feet. Bring the calf we have been fattening and kill it; we are going to have a feast, a celebration, because this son of mine was dead and has come back to life; he was lost and is found." And they began to celebrate. *(Luke 15:22-24)*

Our culture seems different. At airports, train depots and bus stations we repress this kind of affection. We seem to sit on our emotions.

Jesus invites us to move in love and compassion towards others. As well as in the father-son, mother-daughter and interfamilial relationships, Jesus challenges us to reach out to those who hurt us, offend us, reject us. Be present to your enemies, love your enemies, is His startling message.

"But I say this to you who are listening; Love your enemies, do good to those who hate you, bless those who curse you, pray for those who treat you badly. To the man who slaps you on one cheek, present the other cheek too; to the man who takes your cloak from you, do not refuse your tunic. Give to everyone who asks you and do not ask for your property back from the man who robs you. Treat others as you would like them to treat you."

(Luke 6:27-31)

If we begin to love in that way, we will be invited and pulled into the passion of Christ. We will become men and women of compassion. We will be transformed and will have the heart of Christ, the mind of the Father, and the love of the Spirit. We will truly have within ourselves the presence of the Trinity, our loving God.

In fact, our God, the community of the Trinity, from all time wanted to save mankind. In eternal love, in the Divine mind, God decided that Jesus would become Man, that He would live on earth and suffer and die to redeem mankind. Our call is to be co-redeemers with Him.

To call us beyond ourselves even more, He says:

> If you love those who love you, what thanks can you expect? Even sinners love those who love them. And if you do good to those who do good to you, what thanks can you expect? For even sinners do that much. And if you lend to those from whom you hope to receive, what thanks can you expect? Even sinners lend to sinners to get back the same amount. Instead, love your enemies and do good, and lend without any hope of return. You will have a great reward, and you will be sons of the Most High, for he himself is kind to the ungrateful and the wicked.
>
> *(Luke 6:31-35)*

This is a very hard message, but these are the words of Jesus. Some days we will live them; other days we will withdraw. These are His words. This is His invitation. This is the call to enter into the mystery of healing – to be men and women of compassion.

Once we start to move towards another person, towards someone we do not know, we get a reaction. We meet them. We are warm, friendly, affectionate. At least, that is our intention. How do they experience our presence? What messages do we send out? How do they receive us? What is their state of mind? How are they feeling? What do they fear? What is really going on in their consciousness? If we approach a prisoner, a psychiatric patient, a dope addict, a stranger, what will happen? We know we have feelings. So do they. Each person we speak to is also experiencing a multiple feeling reaction in the meeting. We must be aware and sensitive, as we move towards others. We know how different people in our lives affect us. How they change us. We must be conscious that we will also affect others. What a responsibility to one another when we realize we never have a neutral effect on each other. We are invited to co-create and co-redeem each other. A magnificent call to heal!

Dave, a priest I met ten years ago, died in January 1972. One day he said to me, "Don't ever pray to suffer with Christ unless you mean it. He may take you at your word." This man was dying from a brain tumor. When I met him, he was at the peak of his career, aged 44, a spiritual director and writer. All of a sudden cancer struck his brain. I watched him deteriorate for the next three years. In faith, he stayed so present to our community. He kept calling us to be men of compassion. He kept inviting us to know what it meant to suffer for His people. He was doing it. He was a living-death to himself and to us. He was living the ever present Paschal Mystery. One day when he was in Princess Margaret, the cancer hospital in Toronto, he asked me to read this Scripture passage:

Blessed be the God and Father of our Lord Jesus Christ, a gentle Father and the God of all consolation, who comforts us in all our sorrows, so that we can offer others, in their sorrows, the consolation that we have received from God ourselves. Indeed, as the sufferings of Christ overflow to us, so through Christ, does our consolation overflow. When we are made to suffer, it is for your consolation and salvation. When instead, we are comforted, this should be a consolation to you, supporting you in patiently bearing the same sufferings as we bear. And our hope for you is confident, since we know that, sharing our sufferings, you will also share our consolations."

(II Corinthians 1:3-7)

Father Dave rests in my memory as a living-dying compassionate man who called us to be compassionate.

Life is a strange mixture of suffering and joy, good and bad,
pain and peaceful presence.

The suffering of separation at a grandparent's death can evolve into a joyful family reunion.

The marriage of friends is a celebration; a prison sentence,
painful.

A child's honesty is disarming, delightful.

A doctor's truth can limit my life.

Like the popular song we look at life from both sides now, from up and down. . . If we didn't, it would be very depressing. But this is the continuing incarnation of Christ's suffering, death and resurrection. This is the core of His compassion and the ground for our hope.

With the compassionate christ we can easily move towards the eucharist. This breaking of bread, this memorial of the passion, death and resurrection of *the compassionate, gentle healer*, draws us and supports us to live our own personal paschal mystery. We move in the simple yet deeply profound mystery of His presence. It is a time to celebrate and a time to be serious; a time to pray and a time to sing; a time to speak and a time to listen. A time of mixture – another mysterious mixture. So deeply a mystery that as we eat, we grow hungry. As we drink from His cup, we thirst for His life. In the hearing of the Word comes the living of His love. People will even be broken and die for Him and His people just like the fragile bread. What strength we draw from His continued presence!

A prayer:

'Father, we pray that we might grow in compassion and enter deeply into the mystery of the Breaking of Bread. We pray that we might have the mind and heart of your Son, Jesus. We thank you for those times of peace, those moments of Compassion, when we have felt healed because someone has been present to us. We praise you for times when we have been healers, being present to others. We pray that you will increase our sensitivity, soften our hardened hearts, open us so that we can say with your Son:

"How happy are the poor in spirit;
theirs is the kingdom of heaven.
Happy the gentle;
they shall have the earth for their heritage.
Happy those who mourn;
they shall be comforted.
Happy those who hunger and thirst for what is right;
they shall be satisfied.
Happy the merciful;
they shall have mercy shown them.
Happy the pure in heart;
they shall see God.
Happy the peacemakers;
they shall be called sons of God.
Happy those who are persecuted in the cause of right;
theirs is the kingdom of heaven."   *(Matthew 5:3-10)*

We ask you to be with us and deepen our pilgrimage of hope. Take us more profoundly into that mystery which is you.'

To share a banquet with the very rich
        provides possible presence to Him.

            or . . .

To share a meal with poorer folk
        invites an invasion of Spirit.

            or . . .

To share some food with anyone
        harmonizes humans in Him.

            but . . .

To break bread and share the cup
        creates Christians in His Spirit.

a pondering...

select a quiet place...

assume a bodily position...

think...reflect...pray...

What moves in me when I miss someone?

How do I handle separation?   from family,
                                friends,
                                loved ones?

Does death
      desertion
      desolation depress me?

Pain and pestilence,

      War and violence,

            Personal and social suffering abound.

Do I walk away?
    ignore it?
    pretend it's just another TV show?

or,

Do I seek out the suffering person...
    bind up the wounded's wounds...
    absorb their piercing pain...

and become a person of peace
                        of compassionate peace

                                a compassionate healer.

imagine...picture...ponder...

Cure of a leper
> After He had come down from the mountain large crowds
> followed Him. A leper now came up and bowed low in
> front of Him. 'Sir,' he said 'if you want to, you can cure
> me.' Jesus stretched out His hand, touched him and said,
> 'Of course I want to! Be cured!' And his leprosy was cured
> at once. Then Jesus said to him, 'Mind you do not tell
> anyone, but go and show yourself to the priest and make
> the offering prescribed by Moses, as evidence for them'.
> *(Matthew 8:1-4)*

The son of the widow of Nain

Now soon afterwards He went to a town called Nain, accompanied by His disciples and a great number of people. When He was near the gate of the town it happened that a dead man was being carried out for burial, the only son of his mother, and she was a widow. And a considerable number of the townspeople were with her. When the Lord saw her He felt sorry for her. 'Do not cry' He said. Then He went up and put His hand on the bier and the bearers stood still, and He said, 'Young man, I tell you to get up'. And the dead man sat up and began to talk, and Jesus gave him to his mother. Everyone was filled with awe and praised God saying, 'A great prophet has appeared among us; God has visited His people'. And this opinion of Him spread throughout Judaea and all over the countryside.

(Luke 7:11-17)

reflect . . . review . . . live.

THE TENDER HEALER

The word that was addressed to Jeremiah by Jahweh, 'Get
up and make your way down to the potter's house; there I
shall let you hear what I have to say.' So I went down to
the potter's house; and there he was, working at the
wheel. And whenever the vessel he was making came out
wrong, as happens with the clay handled by potters, he
would start afresh and work it into another vessel, as
potters do. Then this word of Yahweh was addressed to
me, 'House of Israel, can not I do to you what this potter
does? – it is Yahweh who speaks. Yes, as the clay is in the
potter's hand, so you are in mine, House of Israel'.

(Jeremiah 18:1-7)

The potter's wheel . . . the clay is soft and supple,
                                    watery and willing.

As the wheel spins, you center the clay,
            hold the clay; it touches you,
                        smudges your hands.
            You feel the spinning wheel.
            You become one with their unity, centered.

Gently, ever so gently, you depress the center of the clay

                        with
                        your
                        thumb.

            You begin to build a side.

                        A simple pot.
                        A fancy ashtray.
                        A delicate vase.

What will emerge?

Creativity happens!

Another potter!

But, a slight slip of the thumb...

you start all over again.

The pot needs to be re-made
and
renewed.

Creatively the potter begins again...centering,
holding,
forming,
moulding,
loving.

To be in the hands of Yahweh, like clay in the potter's hands, is to be supple and free, ready and open, receptive and responsive. To be as easy in His hands as our spirit can be, to be assured that I am held, to know that I am held, is to trust, to believe and to hope. How do we experience ourselves in the Hands of God?

As we move through our theme, which focuses on Jesus, the Healer, and continue to develop the openness to hear His healing voice, to feel His healing touch, sometimes we feel out of harmony with the spin. We experience a warping, an imperfection. Clay does not talk back to the potter at his wheel. The potter's slip warps the bowl or breaks the cup. But the marvel of human creation is that God is our creator, the Divine Potter. In His providence He holds us in His hands and hopes to mould us in His image. He allows us to respond to Him, to say "yes" to His invitation. Sometimes we even say "no!" We do have a choice in living, in knowing and in loving. We do have a responsibility to cooperate, to think and to choose. St. Paul wrote:

> We are God's work of art, created in Christ Jesus to live
> the good life as from the beginning He had meant us to
> live it.   (Ephesians 2:10)

The classic creations of poets, painters and potters stun our imagination with awe. The Piéta calls for more than one viewing; a Rembrandt humbles the heart. Art does reflect the creator. What a work of art when a mother and father help their children grow to become men and women, sons and daughters of God. Indeed, a magnificent work of art!

Works of art help us marvel at the creativity of man. Creation often opens us to the Beyond. Nature faithfully paints four seasons. Mountains etch the sky. Valleys flow with winding rivers. Snow creates a crisp walk in the woods. Rain cools a humid heat haze. Nature stills us. Creation mirrors our God, the Divine Artist.

As men and women created with freedom, we can return thanks to our Creator. Or, we can remain centered in ourselves on the wheel of life. Our responsibility is to flow in love of others. Our attitude is to grow in awareness of others. But, we can forget our responsibility to others and become unaware of the needs around us. We can spin dangerously in isolation.

As we spin, questions emerge. What is happening? Why are we so alone? What are our neighbors' needs? Where will we discover loving relationships? When will our irresponsibility evolve into just action? Will we really change? Who is responsible for our changing?

We are primarily responsible for ourselves. We are God's work of art. We cooperate with the life He has given us from birth. We respond to life situations as we grow through puberty, adolescence, adulthood. It never stops. The *how* of our response is central. We will have many experiences, but will we react positively or negatively? Will we meet life in a mature fashion or in a childish manner? We have choices to make, roads to walk and rivers to cross. In many ways we fashion our own lives. We create our own futures.

The uniqueness of new life that comes forth at birth is a marvelous gift and a stunning responsibility! How do we respond and help to mould our children? How do we love them so that they may emerge as free persons and, at the same time, how do we provide necessary guidance? It would be easy if a child were formed like the clay fingered by the skillful potter or like the figure brushed by a careful painter. How beautiful but inanimate is this form of creation. Compare a 'still life' of Cezanne to a human life – growing, changing, loving. No comparison!

How is the relationship of parent and child during these developing years? The new child changes the new parents. A baby has many needs. The parents learn more ways to be self-sacrificing. Patience, gentleness, joy can all grow. The baby is humanizing the mother and father in new ways, as they call their child to be human. At times the child will need specific directives. As time passes, he must make, and be responsible for, his own decisions. Life choices create bonds and develop friendships.

Something beautiful exists when children can meet their grandparents and have a special relationship with them. What a great thing it is in a family where the old and the young discover the beauty of each other. What a gift when parents set the stage, encourage and foster all this to happen! To have human clay in our hands is a beautiful but awesome responsibility. Parents are indeed potters.

What about those who have chosen to live a different life? Where does the single man and woman come into this? Where does the nun, priest or person called to celibacy take part in the creation of new life? These people also desire to be co-creators, living in relationships that call to new life. The human spirit instinctually fosters and parents human life. The High School teacher assumes the role of surrogate father or mother for many adolescents, as does a nurse, a Sister or a drop-in director. The priest or minister can be a parent in many ways. All men and women, single or celibate, married or not, move in parenting relationships. Our roles can be healing or hurting, productive or crushing. Whether we are the natural father or the science teacher, the caring mother or the concerned doctor, the pastor or the cross-walk attendant, the cashier at the Supermarket or the laborer at the construction site, we all need a serious outlook. The clay of youth is in our hands.

Our own values, beliefs, attitudes mould the lives of others. We are a part of all that we have met. We enrich from the wealth of our enrichment. We give from the gifts we have received. We share our knowledge, our talents, our abilities from what we have learned, received, accepted. We glaze the minds and hearts of others with our love and hope. Or, we marr their spirits with confusion; we crack their hope with harshness; we fire their minds with false ideas. We have power to build up or tear down. We can handle with care or smack. We have a grave responsibility. The future is important and in a real sense, we are the future.

We are our total life experience – infant, child, adolescent, adult. We are not always just one of these but sometimes all of them. How do we respond at each level? Do we love the infant in us? Can we accept those moments when the gangling adolescent still appears? To be attentive to the child in each of us is important. The Father knows we all have the 'child' stirring within us. He is so gentle with us. He understands our hopes and desires. Maybe we muse: "Will someone hold me?...embrace me, when times are tough?...will a gentle arm support me?" Through gentleness and tenderness we begin to feel accepted and loved. We open up a bit and put our hand out to that person who will take it. We dare to trust. We do this when we really believe that no matter where in life we find ourselves, no matter which way He moulds the clay, the Father will do it in a loving way. He calls us to love because He loves us. This means risks, relationships, openness and dialogue. It will mean pain too, and healing. It will move us to be gentle because we are loved. It will make us compassionate and draw us to those who suffer, as painful as they may be. We will also become healers.

To be a co-creator with the Father in answering the call to co-mould human life in the image and likeness of God is His invitation to each one of us. As we enter human relationships, engage in personal friendships and meet problems head-on, we animate change both in ourselves and in others. We humanize and divinize our world through a responsible attitude to an evolution of the human condition.

Another way

During the winter of 1972 Pat and Jo began to experience interior rumblings. Even with a successful business and three young and beautiful children the desire to change was surfacing. Thoughts of service to the poor, assisting the handicapped whether mental or physical, and the words of Jesus, "Go, sell what you have and come follow me," kept challenging their life-style. It seems foolish to give up a good job with a lucrative salary and live on slender means with an extension of the family to include some poorer men and women of our culture. But they did! They sold out, packed their bags and moved. A struggling pilgrimage ensued.

Life was so different in the beginning. Some friends lent them a house on the edge of the city, but it needed repair. The family grew from five to seven when two mentally-handicapped men came to live with them. Volunteers came to help but soon some left; others stayed on. They were short on money so Pat worked as a janitor in the nearby school. Jo cooked, scrubbed and baked to make ends meet. More handicapped arrived. A couple of volunteers stayed for over a year. The community was growing, paining and learning to celebrate.

To live in this extended family, this new form of community, called them to new life. Some people thought they were crazy; others admired them greatly. The children sometimes wondered what was happening but grew in a unique kind of openness. One day, with a tear in her eye, the youngest quizzed: 'Why are they with us?' The struggle for time with their children, the community, and of course with each other, caused tension. Facing these difficulties through community discussions and personal exchanges called everyone to grow through the suffering and appreciate the joyful

CATHY

I met a pilgrim in a northern land
Who ached: Each deep and timeless touch of Lourdes
rests in her heart. With me, in the room,
half-hurt, a furrowed face smiles, whose frown
and frightened look, and fear of friends around,
tells me my friend will need a gentle hand
which will retouch, rekindle the wounded parts;
the word that shocked her and the hand that smacked.
But in her eyes the message is clear:
"My name is Cathy, a child of the universe,
look on my life, you people, and have hope!"
Everything inside me stirs. Wrapped round in love
by this community, caring with concern,
a slow but sure beginning surges forth.

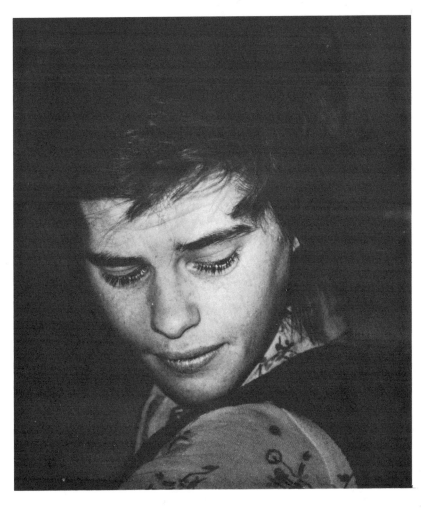

She turned and wept quietly,
because someone had pointed
a finger at her.

moments even more deeply. They learned that the human spirit explodes in joy almost in proportion that it can endure pain and suffering.

During these five years the community has expanded to two houses with one centered around the family and the other directed by two single people. Each numbers about twelve people; they operate independently but often join forces for an outing or a birthday party. The quality of openness, the ability to share their meals with strangers, the definite stance of welcoming, all point to people responding to life in a radical gospel way. They incarnate the Beatitudes. They live the meaning of "When I was hungry, you gave me to eat. When I was thirsty, you gave me to drink. When I was a stranger you welcomed me." *(Matthew 25:35)* They challenge and invite; they encourage and cajole; and we wonder: 'what about me?'

Jesus' first community

A quiet reading of Matthew's Infancy Narratives (Chapters 1 & 2) presents the family of Jesus from Joseph's viewpoint. This revelation unfolds the heart of Joseph's faith life. He lived his life on four dreams. Martin Luther King once said "I had a dream"...well, Joseph had four. The first said: "Yes, accept Mary, it's all right. Do not be afraid." He believed. Imagine if you were about to be married and you discovered that your wife was pregnant. But more striking, imagine if you quietly received a prayerful message that the Holy Spirit was responsible for the conception. The pregnancy was a miracle! Joseph, the faith-filled man, complied, believed and lived out his call. The other dreams led him. When Herod threatened the Infant Jesus' life, Joseph dreamed: "Get up, take the child and his mother with you, and escape into Egypt and stay there until I tell you..." *(Matthew 2:13)* Joseph again was obedient. Some time later, after Herod had died, the Lord Yahweh communicated with Joseph again. This time the words of his dream were: "Get up, take the child and his mother with you and go back to the land of Israel, for those who wanted to kill the child are dead." *(Matthew 2:20)* Joseph heard the message and returned to his fatherland. While on the journey, he feared Archelaus, Herod's son, so he went to Galilee having been inspired by another dream-revelation. *(Matthew 2:22)* (Scripturally and theologically, the dream is a medium of communication of the Spirit to man.) The messages came to Joseph. He listened in his very being; he loved with all his heart; he discerned, made choices and acted. His life invites us into that kind of decision-making.

If you want to go on a beautiful pilgrimage, wander through Luke's Infancy Narratives with Mary. (Chapters 1 & 2) See the genealogy and the heritage. Hear the dialogue. Watch the people...Mary, Elizabeth, Zacharias. Observe their actions. Enter the mystery. Mary must have sat and chatted with Luke, telling him about family things and sharing intimate details. Can you imagine the feelings in her heart when she talks about Jesus being born. She gave birth in a stable. How humbling that must have been. But isn't Mary the gentle one?

When we are humbled, how gentle we can become. How sensitive, strong but supple, willing and waiting...we can evolve. Sometimes we want to operate out of power and control. We even want to dominate or manipulate. What's frightening is that sometimes we do not even know we are doing it. Our awareness is zero!

Suddenly something happens – a word, a gesture, an event. We receive some kind of humiliation. We flash with feelings of embarrassment. We blush, hesitate, fumble. With God's grace we realize that a gift is being given. The humiliation calls us to grow in humility. We feel the urge to be tender in our relationships. We are gentled. Stilled. Humbled.

A loving relationship

There was a man named Lazarus who lived in the village of Bethany with the two sisters, Mary and Martha, and he was ill. It was the same Mary, the sister of the sick man Lazarus, who anointed the Lord with ointment and wiped his feet with her hair. The sisters sent this message to Jesus, 'Lord, the man you love is ill.' On receiving the message, Jesus said, 'The sickness will end not in death but in God's glory, and through it the Son of God will be glorified.' Jesus loved Martha and her sister and Lazarus."
(John 11:1-5)

"The man you love is ill." When a man loves, he really cares. When he makes a commitment in love, sees clearly what he is called to, then he moves. Jesus loved with deep human conviction. He always said: "Let the children come to me." *(Mark 10:14)* "Come to Me all you who labour and are heavy burdened, and I will give you rest. Shoulder my yoke and learn from me, for I am gentle and humble in heart." *(Matthew 11:28-30)* "I give you a new commandment: Love one another; just as I have loved you, you also must love one another." *(John 13:34)* Jesus lived his life in relationships of love.

In His humanity Jesus really loved. His heart beat with love like any other man. His affections were strong and deep. He felt His love for people. He had friends, close friends. This love was not purely platonic, and intellectual love. His love was full, from every fiber of His being.

When Christ told His disciples that they should leave for Judea to see Lazarus, they were anxious because His enemies wanted to stone Him. He replied:

"Are there not twelve hours in the day? A man can walk in the daytime without stumbling because he has the light of this world to see by; but if he walks at night he stumbles, because there is no light to guide him."

(Jn. 11.9-10)

Jesus truly loved Lazarus and moved toward him. He knew that the light of His Father and the Spirit was with Him so He could return despite the opposition, despite all that was happening. He knew it was time to return because it would glorify the Father. Besides, His friends needed Him.

Whether we are single or married, priest or sister, old or young, rich or poor, whoever we are and in whatever way we are committed to love, we will need the light of God. We will need the light of Christ. We will need His mind, His Heart, to love in His way. We will need time to ponder, muse and pray, since love does not stop with thoughts and feelings. It moves to action and service, honesty and fidelity, openness and dialogue. We need this interior movement, the spirit of Jesus, to grow in this orientation of our lives.

Jesus then said to His disciples:

"Our friend Lazarus is resting, I am going to wake him." The disciples said to him, "Lord, if he is able to rest he is sure to get better." The phrase Jesus used referred to the death of Lazarus, but they thought that by "rest" he meant "sleep", so Jesus put it plainly. "Lazarus is dead;

and for your sake I am glad I was not there because now
you will believe. But let us go to him." Then Thomas,
known as the Twin, said to the other disciples, "Let us go
too, and die with him."   *(John 11:11-16)*

To see Jesus   is to see love.

          moving   his friend
                    towards Lazarus

There is something about love that cuts down all barriers. It holds
something so strong that it takes a person beyond even his own
bindings. Whatever the pain, we are not stopped by it, but move
with love. Personal problems do not paralyse love. Rather, love
motivates us to risk a new relationship, remain faithful to an old
one, resolve disputes and disagreements, build and develop friendships, be gentle, patient and kind. Each one of us is called to love
each day.

It is not a question of all of us rushing off to help in the Third
World. We are not going to do that. In fact, we are probably not
called to this. There may be some called to this service for sometimes
a heart is stirred and a person desires to live and love in another
culture. But this is a very personal call.

Given our present life situation with all its responsibilities, each
one of us must ask himself: "How am I to live the Gospel here in
St. Louis or Sydney, Washington or Windsor? How will my life incarnate love like Jesus did? How will I love my neighbor?"

It is not a matter of stepping out
                                        in order to
                    step over
                                        who is there, but it is
          a matter
                    of meeting the person.
          We do not step out to
                    step over, but
                    step forward,
                         into, and
                         around. . .and

                                        we are present.

83

There is so much pain around us,
an aching in all.
Cultures are shifting; countries are struggling;
families are paining; individuals are suffering;
the change and flux is gigantic.
What do we do?
There is a natural tendency to avoid pain,
to pop a pill for everything,
to ignore suffering in others,
to withdraw,
to build my own little world.
There is another stirring in our heart,
another call from within to with-out.
There is another invitation to live, not just with, but beyond
personal pain.
to work, not just for the outcast, but
to love him.

ebb and flow . . .
ascending and descending . . .
in and out . . .
to pray about,
around,
through these sufferings.

Peter and Thomas, Jesus' friends, had to face suffering. They were determined to go to Calvary with Jesus. He prophesied His sufferings; they watched the flow of events; confusion, question, doubt, but friendship kept them close for a time. They watched at a distance.

We too will be called to death, a death to ourselves. We die to our selfishness, ego-centrism, sin, in order to live. We ask for the Spirit of Jesus so we can say with St. Paul, "I live now, not I, but Christ lives in me." *(Galatians 2:20)* Our call is to sometimes let another person put their hands on the clay of our heart, tenderly taking that clay and forming, moulding and helping us. At other times, we hold their heart in our hands. The clay of a person's heart often sticks to our hands. They leave us something of themselves; they too walk away with a part of us. We each must learn to love and be loved, to trust and be trusted, to hold and be held, to suffer with and for each other. It is only when we die to self, become poor in spirit and truly try to become like Jesus, that we will be able to truly reach out and love, whether in pain or in joy. The call of Jesus, Martha and Mary is our call. . . to move in the light, to love.

> On arriving, Jesus found that Lazarus had been in the tomb for four days already. When Martha heard that Jesus had come she went to meet Him. Mary remained sitting in the house. Martha said to Jesus, 'If you had been here, my brother would not have died, but I know that, even now, whatever you ask of God, he will grant you.'
>
> 'Your brother,' said Jesus to her, 'will rise again.' Martha said, 'I know he will rise again at the resurrection on the last day.' Jesus said:
>
> 'I am the Resurrection. If anyone believes in me, even though he dies he will live, and whoever lives and believes in me will never die. Do you believe this?'
>
> 'Yes Lord', she said, 'I believe that you are the Christ, the Son of God, the one who was to come into this world.'
>
> *(John 11:17-27)*

We ask that we too might believe in a resurrection, that we too might respond with Mary in faith, in strength and in belief. With a living faith we desire to love more tenderly, more deeply.

When she had said this, she went and called her sister
Mary, saying in a low voice, 'The Master is here and
wants to see you.' Hearing this, Mary got up
quickly...Mary went to Jesus, and as she saw him she
threw herself at his feet, saying, 'Lord, if you had been
here, my brother would not have died.' At the sight of her
tears, and those of the Jews who followed her, Jesus said
in great distress, with a sigh that came straight from the
heart, 'Where have you put him?' They said, 'Lord, come
and see.' Jesus wept, and the Jews said, 'See how much he
loved him!'   *(John 11:18-37)*

Jesus wept! Those two words strike me so strongly. Jesus, so fully
human and divine, can weep. He can have that much love for
Lazarus, Martha and Mary. When a man or woman weeps because
they love, it is very real, true and often painful. In our culture we are
programmed, over programmed in our feelings. The culture has told
us so often how we are to feel. Are we free in ourselves to show our
true feelings when we love, when we care? The call for each of us is
the same mystery of love—

> living and dying,
> > giving and receiving,
> > > aching and rejoicing,
> of having sighs that come straight from our hearts,
> of feeling the cost and the joy of love.

Still sighing, Jesus reached the tomb: it was a cave with a
stone to close the opening. Jesus said, 'Take the stone
away.' Martha said to him, 'Lord, by now he will smell;
this is the fourth day.' Jesus replied, 'Have I not told
you that if you believe you will see the glory of God?' So
they took away the stone. Then Jesus lifted up his eyes
and said:

'Father, I thank you for hearing my prayer. I knew indeed that you always hear me, but I speak for the sake of
all these who stand around me, so that they may believe it
was you who sent me.'

When he had said this, he cried in a loud voice,
'Lazarus, here! Come out!' The dead man came out, his

feet and hands bound with bands of stuff and a cloth around his face. Jesus said to them, 'Unbind him, let him go free.' (John II:38-44)

The tenderness of Jesus is evident in this chapter of John's Gospel. He can weep. He can sigh. He can say: "I am the Resurrection and the Life!" He can give hope. He can show concern and form solid, human relationships. As He moved into these relationships, each one differed because He was human, fully man and fully God. In that mystery He comes to say to us: "Come, follow Me, in love and tenderness. Be present to other people – your husband, your wife, your neighbor, the members of your community, the pastor in the adjoining parish, the reject, the isolate, the lonely." Jesus wants us to be tender. Tenderness is present in a touch, a word, in silence. It can soften a heart of steel, still a ranting rage and calm a fearful frown. Tenderness is incarnated love springing from the heart. It is a touch of eternity in time.

As we reflect, mull over and pray, His spirit moves in us to relate with each other with the same acceptance and tenderness of Jesus. Is that not our desire? Do we not hope to be like Jesus, the Gentle One the Tender One,
the Healer.

To be a person of tenderness can be so healing to others, and indeed to ourselves. Let us move in tender ways for more tender times.

Prayer:

Lord, we pray that we will be open to be men and women of tenderness, love and kindness. Create within us stronger desires for compassion, gentleness and tenderness. Call us to be the Light of the World. Teach us to speak when it is time, to be still, to be silent in solitude when it is time. Give us the tenderness of Your Son. Teach us to weep, to laugh, to pain and dance with your people. Call us to fullness of life and freedom, freedom to love and freedom to believe. Lord, teach us to pray. At times it is a cold and long December kind of day. Teach us to pray, to hope. Lord . . . teach us to Love! to be tender!

A bustling day quiets before crackling logs,
sit...pray...
A sudden thought leaps to a receptive mind,
pray...reject...
A growing awareness urges to a possible response,
ponder...pray...
A quiet lady unites with a moving spirit,
touched...yes!

The day calls for a timely visit,
helping...giving...
The thought grows in a stronger way,
firming...confirming...
The awareness enfleshes in a real person,
breathing...moving...
The lady presents a special child,
crying...loving...

Days pass to weeks, to months,
watch...pray...feel...
Thoughts roam from person to person,
read...reflect...pray...
Awareness flows and goes again,
prayer...strong...real...
My lady mulls over her life,
strange...growth...spirit...

But the day dawns for death,
pondered...often.
And the thought of separation,
finalized...now.
And the awareness of growth,
agonized...here.
But my lady hopes in life,
resurrected...yes!

A pondering . . .

read . . . muse . . . mull over.

Anointing of His feet
Six days before the Passover, Jesus went to Bethany,
where Lazarus was, whom he had raised from the dead.
They gave a dinner for him there; Martha waited on
them and Lazarus was among those at table. Mary
brought in a pound of very costly ointment, pure nard,
and with it anointed the feet of Jesus, wiping them with
her hair; the house was full of the scent of the ointment.
Then Judas Iscariot – one of his disciples, the man who
was to betray him – said, 'Why wasn't this ointment sold
for three hundred denarii, and the money given to the
poor?' He said this, not because he cared about the poor,
but because he was a thief; he was in charge of the common fund and used to help himself to the contributions.
So Jesus said, 'Leave her alone; she had to keep this scent
for the day of my burial. You have the poor with you
always, you will not always have me.'   (John 12:1-8)

Jesus and the children

> People brought little children to him, for him to lay his hands on them and say a prayer. The disciples turned them away, but Jesus said, 'Let the little children alone, and do not stop them coming to me; for it is to such as these that the kingdom of heaven belongs'. Then he laid his hands on them and went on his way.

(Matthew 19:13-15)

Eating with sinners

> When Jesus was at dinner in his house, a number of tax collectors and sinners were also sitting at the table with Jesus and his disciples; for there were many of them among his followers. When the scribes of the Pharisee party saw him eating with sinners and tax collectors, they said to his disciples, 'Why does he eat with tax collectors and sinners?' When Jesus heard this he said to them, 'It is not the healthy who need the doctor, but the sick. I did not come to call the virtuous, but sinners.'

(Mark 2:15-17)

The widow's mite

As he looked up he saw rich people putting their offerings into the treasury; then he happened to notice a poverty-stricken widow putting in two small coins, and he said, 'I tell you truly, this poor widow has put in more than any of them; for these have all contributed money they had over, but she from the little she had has put in all she had to live on'. *(Luke 21:1-4)*

recall...renew...wonder about.

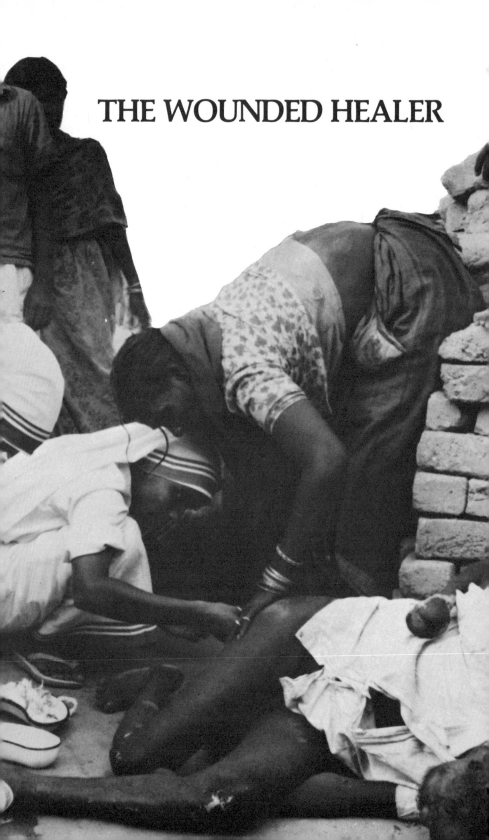

THE WOUNDED HEALER

To speak of Jesus as the Wounded Healer is to focus on His healing by His wounds and eventually by His death. The climax of healing is in the death of Jesus Christ on Calvary. His death is the moment of freedom, the moment of truth. Jesus' passing-over is the love of our God-made-Man consummated, completed and given for us. It is this paschal mystery which we have heard about many times – the passion, death and resurrection of Jesus. In this moment He releases His Spirit for ultimate healing.

We feel His love at the last supper when He says to His disciples, "I have longed to eat this meal with you before I suffer." *(Luke 22:15)* This will be their last passover meal. This will be the last time they gather to share, eat and drink together. At the third blessing cup Jesus will break bread and give them His body. He will bless the wine and give them His blood. This Jewish ritual meal will become the first Eucharist.

His deep love and desire to be with them overflows into an act of service.

> They were at supper, and the devil had already put it into the mind of Judas Iscariot son of Simon, to betray him. Jesus knew that the Father had put everything into his hands, and that he had come from God and was returning to God, and he got up from table, removed his outer garment and, taking a towel, wrapped it around his waist; he then poured water into a basin and began to wash the disciples' feet and to wipe them with the towel he was wearing." *(John 13:2-5)*

Jesus acts contrary to custom. A servant's job is to wash the master's feet. He reverses the traditional practice. He upsets the routine. His disciples were amazed, disturbed and confused. We know that happened with Peter, the impetuous Peter.

'Lord, are you going to wash my feet?' Jesus answered, 'At the moment you do not know what I am doing, but later you will understand.' 'Never!' said Peter. 'You shall never wash my feet.' Jesus replied, 'If I do not wash you, you can have nothing in common with me.' 'Then, Lord,' said Simon Peter, 'not only my feet, but my hands and my head as well!' Jesus said, 'No one who has taken a bath needs washing, he is clean all over. You too are clean, though not all of you are.' He knew who was going to betray him, that was why he said, 'though not all of you are.' When he had washed their feet and put on his clothes again he went back to the table. 'Do you understand,' he said, 'what I have done to you? You call me Master and Lord, and rightly; so I am. If I, then, the Lord and Master, have washed your feet, you should wash each other's feet. I have given you an example so that you may copy what I have done to you. 'I tell you most solemnly, no servant is greater than his master, no messenger is greater than the man who sent him. Now that you know this, happiness will be yours if you behave accordingly.'

(John 13:6-17)

How will we wash each others feet?
How will we be servants, waiters, dish-washers?
How will we love our neighbor?
our teacher? the cabbie? the bus driver?
the porter? the policeman?
our enemy? who? where? why?
As Jesus said: THIS IS MY COMMANDMENT:
LOVE ONE ANOTHER, AS I HAVE LOVED YOU.

Some people work as nurses. Bed baths, injections, back rubs are but a few moments of washing feet. Some are mothers. Many times you have washed your children, changed the little ones and fed them. Others work with adolescents, alcoholics, aged. Men work, sometimes they moonlight, to feed and clothe their family. A gentle but firm hand often must arbitrate wranglings, budget tensions and traffic snarls. To wash other people with the water of gentleness, to bathe them with the water of tenderness, to serve them with love and concern is to wash their feet like Jesus, the Healer. The thrust is simple – discover the creative possibilities of washing the feet of our friends.

There are many levels of the *commitment to service*. It may be a passing moment or a lasting situation. A friend comes for a weekend, but you live on in your family. The visitor washes feet in one way, but you are continually with your family. You will wash their feet in a very different way. The kind of commitment that endures day to day is much deeper and lasts much longer. They are not to be compared. They are different from, or better than! The quality of the service is what counts. Jesus tells us that happiness will be ours if we do this. He invites us to the ordinary, day-to-day, rountine washing of feet.

Some people find it strange when a visitor comes to their home and offers to help with the dishes. It is a great gift to allow your visitors into your kitchen to make a piece of toast or brew a cup of coffee. It is meaningful when a friendship changes from the polite living room parlance "how do you do?" to the chatter of the kitchen table. We no longer need a fancy tablecloth, just two mugs for tea or coffee. We are becoming friends. The little services that we render means that it is real. It is no longer a tea party. It is a friendship. At some point we will really begin to love each other – with its sharing, sacrifice, cost and joy.

Once people start to love and trust each other, they begin to open their hearts. They quickly discover that almost everyone carries a wound of some kind. Somewhere in the recesses of their heart there is a hurt. This does not mean that they are immersed in depression, that all is terrible or that they cannot live life. Most of us carry something of the wound of life that will come through to the resurrection. Many realize their need for clarification by the Light of the World. Darkness calls for light. Most recognize the need to be transformed in His glorified hands like the clay of the potter. Once we start to accept whom we are and stop comparing ourselves with everyone else, we can say, maybe in a whisper: "I'm me and you know what . . . God loves me as I am! He accepts me!" We can then begin to let Him lance the wound that might be covered over and even festering a little. We can trust enough to let the Surgeon get at it with His scalpel. Sometimes this means just talking about the wound. At other times it means accepting the pain. Or, it may mean tears, a scream, forgiveness. The movement of the friendship grows and develops. The Spirit is its cutting edge – prompting, urging, guiding.

In 1973 while I was working at Jesu Ashram, a hospital for the destitute-poor near Siliguri, India, I met Gopel. During those memorable days, I wrote this: "Three days ago I visited Koila Depot Busti on the edge of Siliguri which is about four hundred miles north of Calcutta. I met many people there, but I want to share a friend with you. He is Gopel, a young boy of five, who lives in a small thatched-roof house in the middle of the village. His parents, as do most of their neighbors, make their living by burning off charcoal from the coal and reselling it to vendors in the streets.

"The village itself is dirty and smoke filled. The pathways between the houses are smooth and firm from the many barefooted people who carry coal in baskets on their heads. Their thin bodies, dust-caked hands and feet, and dirty clothing are all signs of their occupation.

"But let us come back to Gopel. He was standing there smiling when I met him. I said a couple of words to him in Hindi but later found that he was Nepali. Thus our communication was, and is, non-verbal. He was shy when I first met him but our friendship has deepened. After we bought him a little pair of red shorts I took him on the bus to our hospital for the destitute about three miles from Siliguri, carrying him from the bus stop. Gopel was used to being carried so he curled his legs around my waist and clasped his arms around my neck as I walked down the road to Jesu Ashram.

"Most of the kids at the hospital are there because their parents are sick, but we do have one orphan. We introduced Gopel to them all and, although they shied away from him in the beginning, he has become good friends with Delip, Subash, Sunita, and the others. He has been eating well and smiling a lot since he has been with us. However, he does want to go home and because he is not really sick he will leave in a couple of days.

"Last night touched my heart. I walked into the ward where he stays, and when he saw me, he ran as fast to meet me as his spindly little legs allowed. I lifted him up and held him for a long time. We don't talk much but we do communicate.

"Gopel is a lively high-spirited little boy. He chatters away like any five-year old. He loves to rough house and be picked up and swung around. The only difference is that he has only one foot. His other foot was cut off by a train and the doctors amputated just below the ankle. He has a round stub and with a sponge pad and a cloth covering it, he can really get around."

Gopel received an artificial limb in the fall of '73. At first he had a hard time adjusting, but now he walks well.

How does Christ handled His sufferings?

> They came to a small estate called Gethsemane, and Jesus said to his disciples, 'Stay here while I pray.' Then he took Peter and James and John with him. And a sudden fear came over him, and great distress. And he said to them, 'My soul is sorrowful to the point of death. Wait here, and keep awake.' And going on a little further he threw himself on the ground and prayed that, if it were possible, this hour might pass him by. 'Abba (Father)!', he said. 'Everything is possible for you. Take this cup away from me. But let it be as you, not I, would have it.'
>
> ((Mark 14:32-37)

There are many forms of fear in our world...
    fear of the unknown,

        of other people,

      fear of sickness,

           suffering,

                death!

fear of being wounded, physically,
                emotionally,
                psychologically.

fear of sharing,
      loving,
          giving,
             receiving,
                opening.
fear of touching
    or
  being touched

of holding
    or
  being held

of meeting
    or
  being met.

fear can cripple, paralyse, deaden.

AND JESUS WAS FEARFUL!

In His humanity he feared. It says in one translation that His sweat became as drops of blood. He knew that it would take this wound of death to redeem mankind. His love would cost Him His life.

Jesus was in distress in the Garden of Gethsemane. He was suffering. Do we not feel moments of . . .

> distress?
>> anguish?
>>> fear?
>>> loneliness?
>>>> isolation?
>>>>> separation?

When some fear grips us, we remember that the
> Wounded Healer knew fear.

When we feel rejected,
> ignored,
> deserted, we remember that the
> Wounded Healer loves us.

Whatever our pain or wound may be, He can heal us because He has been there too. His prayer was: **"Is there another way Father that we can redeem the world? If so, I would like to do it in another way!"** All seems to be dry and dead, hopeless and meaningless. He is very much alone. But Jesus also said:

"Not my will, but yours be done Father!"   *(Mark 14:37)*

He waited . . .
> Time passed, a long time!
>> . . . anguish deepened.
>> . . . aloneness sharpened.
>> . . . fear increased.

He thinks . . .
> "I'll go back and try to get some consolation
> from my friends."
. . . He found them sleeping.

He said to Simon Peter:

> "Simon, are you asleep? Had you not the strength to keep
> awake one hour? You should be awake, and praying not
> to be put to the test."   *(Mark 14:37)*

He goes to his friends and they are asleep. Then He makes that
profound statement – *"the spirit is willing but the flesh is weak."*
(Mark 14:38) How often we feel that! How often we have desires,
promptings to act, to move...but!!! The 'buts', 'ifs' and 'maybes'
flood in. So the flesh is weak, and we have to accept it. So we are
weak and we need His love, His healing. Sometimes we operate
from a point of vulnerability – then, His strength comes through.
St. Paul grasped the reality, *"for when I am weak, then I am strong."*
                                                            (II Cor. 12:10)

We know what Jesus wants. We move, move forward in Him. We
pass through the suffering. The Wounded Healer heals us again. He
calls us to be fellow-wounded-Healers. It is not the person who is
perfectly healthy who comes to heal the other person. It is not the
person who 'has it all together' who can help the person who does
not. Often we come seeking a facile answer but there is none. We
seek someone with whom to share. We chat. Sometimes we get a
glimpse, half an answer for ourselves. Many times we find that they
too are wounded. They too have a pain. Maybe that is why they
understand. It is not exactly the same pain because we are all so
unique. We know that the person has suffered something in some
way but the Spirit has touched and healed him. The healing does not
mean becoming totally whole but entering the process toward
wholeness. We are on the way. We are getting well. Our whole life is
convalescing in Christ. It is a continual healing, a continual coming
to health. It is a movement to the Father, doing His will, knowing
the heart of Jesus, His Son, and led by the Spirit of love.

At the Garden they are asleep again when Jesus comes back.

> And once more he came back and found them sleeping,
> their eyes were so heavy; and they could find no answer
> for him. He came back a third time and said to them, 'You
> can sleep on now and take your rest. It is all over. The
> hour has come. Now the Son of Man is to be betrayed into
> the hands of sinners. Get up! Let us go! My betrayer is
> close at hand already.'   *(Mark 14:39-42)*

Judas, the betrayer, comes. They capture Him, lead Him away. Where are his friends who sat at the Passover meal, whose feet He washed? It is so hard because they are so human. They are so much like us; we like them. When the going gets tough, we pull back because without the Spirit we are weak. Just as they needed Pentecost to live the faith and proclaim that 'Jesus is Lord', so we too need the Spirit.

Our world sleeps. Nations forget the message of love when they demand tariffs too high from Third World countries. Countries depleting the natural resources of others refuse to remember what a just wage is. Statistics startle us when we realize that 6% of the world's population is living off 40% of the world's goods. As the nations of Namibia and Zimbabwe awake, bloodshed and killing mark the process of justice. Racial struggles within countries, just land claims for the native peoples of North America, needed and necessary prison reform, etc. all speak of a sleeping world.

"I'm going to follow and see what happens. . .at a distance." (Mark 14:54) Peter stayed around. Which one of us does not know what happened to Peter?

While Peter was down below in the courtyard, one of the high priest's servant girls came up. She saw Peter warming himself there, stared at him and said, 'You too were with Jesus, the man from Nazareth.' But he denied it. 'I do not know, I do not understand, what you are talking about.'   (Mark 14:66-68)

The Spirit moved in Peter. He repented, went out and wept bitterly. Can you imagine the emotional upheaval in Peter? At times do we not go through this same kind of upheaval?

The pain of the person wounded psychologically may pierce us. He suffers because life does not have any meaning. He cannot find out why. He does not understand. Nobody loves him and how much he aches! How much we have to be present to him. He brings us the wounded Christ. He is so present in His wounds around us. We pray for eyes to see Him, ears to hear His cry. As we move into relationships with these people, they will sometimes heal us. They have withdrawn! They are in His passion. They invite us to meet the suffering Christ. One day we will both pass over to the resurrection. "What a gift, what a grace, they have been!" we will ponder.

Jesus goes before the Sanhedrin, the Jewish court.

"SPEAK"

As we imagine the scene, we see the officials and Jesus, bound. We hear their questions, the slap across His face. Sometimes, if we pray quietly, we can feel the slap. We can sense His embarrassment. We know His determination.

Jesus goes before Pilate, the Roman governor.

...SILENCE...

Again, we see the scene. Questions come but no response. 'Who is this man?' Pilate wonders. His wife tries to tip him off. Somehow she knew. The confusion...the anger...the frustration...and Jesus remained peaceful.

"My Kingdom is not of this world!"   *(John 18:36)*

He is not interested in power, in wealth, in possessions. He embraces humility, meekness, patience. He lives all these marvelous gifts of the Spirit.

This is the kingdom in which He wants us to live. He invites us to be men and women of compassion, to be able to suffer with people; or, He simply asks us to be present when people pain. For example, we sit with a loved one who is dying. We console a family torn by separation. Perhaps all we can do is hold their hand because words do not explain the loss. Our presence may heal or at least hold the pain. We tend the bruises.

Jesus carries His cross

LOVE

Pilate orders a scourging. He picks up His cross and moves towards Calvary. Who is there? Who meets Him along the way? Who is faithful? His Mother! – the woman who pondered these things in her heart. *(Luke 2:33-35)* She gave birth to Him in Bethlehem's stable. She lived out her commitment. How painful that must have been! Sometime, if you ever get the opportunity, go into a barn, sit down and imagine giving birth to a child in that stark simplicity. Or, imagine how Joseph felt. His wife, His foster child, the mysterious Messiah. Both Mary and Joseph had wondered and pondered. Mary has come to see Him hang and die. She sees the wound in His side gashed by the lance. She must have looked into His eyes and seen the love, the desire He had for His people, for us. And His love for her...

Seeing his mother and the disciple he loved standing near her, Jesus said to his mother, 'Woman, this is your son.' Then to the disciple he said, 'This is your mother.' And from that moment the disciple made a place for her in his home." *(John 19:26-27)*

He looks after His mother at the moment of His death. His love transcends His own sufferings. We need His spirit to be able to live like this. It is a real sign of His presence when we can love and transcend ourselves, when we can die to ourselves, and give life to others. Christ's sufferings and death are present with us in many paining people. Many times we tend to withdraw and pull back because it reminds us of our own sufferings and death. We have such a zest for life that we do not want to meet suffering and yet, we know we have been healed when we have opened ourselves to someone else's suffering. We enter the mystery of suffering. We touch the suffering person. Often we are touched, healed, helped. They minister to us.

Jesus is mocked

The passers-by jeered at him; they shook their heads and said, 'Aha! So you would destroy the Temple and rebuild it in three days! Then save yourself: Come down from the cross!' The chief priests and the scribes mocked him among themselves in the same way. 'He saved others,' they said, 'he cannot save himself. Let the Christ, the King of Israel, come down from the cross now, for us to see it and believe.' Even those who were crucified with him taunted him. *((Mark 15:29-32)*

It is the Father's Will. Jesus will stay on the cross. He will die for us. He will cry out the beginning of the 22nd psalm:

"My God, My God why have you forsaken me?"

and finally He will breathe His last and give up His spirit.

JESUS DIES...NEW LIFE!'

Mankind is redeemed. The Church is born. In that moment of truth, when He died, the gates of heaven are opened. The Son has re-established the ultimate love relationship with the Father. The doors are open to all men. Jesus and the Father can send the Holy Spirit. Pentecost can happen. The Spirit can come. Love can invade the world, the heart of man.

Wounded hands speak so softly
of hours, days, months,
of waiting...open.

Wounded hands question quietly
of how, what, when,
of coming...soon.

Wounded hands reach reverently
for love, life, laughter,
for Lord...too.

Wounded hands touched tenderly
by Heart, Host, Heaven,
by Him...often.

Wounded hands wait watchfully
for His coming,
for Her Lord,
for Him.

Wounded hands...Christina's hands,
Christina's world,
Christina's Lord.

Jesus is taken down.
. . . Friendship . . .

Joseph of Arimathea and Nicodemus, who came by night, took His body down from the cross and placed it in the tomb. They sealed the tomb and went home. It was Friday, the eve of Sabbath. From sundown on Friday until sunrise on Sunday, they prayed; they waited; they were fearful.

Sometimes some of us are in a tomb. We are not sure when we will rise. We wait. There are moments of life, flashes of hope and at times we have great expectancy. But there are times when we are in the tomb with the stone rolled shut. We do not know exactly how we will rise. But Jesus rose. We know that we will rise. We have hope.

There are the days when we are back on the cross or in the garden with His agony. 'What is God's will for me? How can I tell in the concrete situation of my life if this is what God wants?' I pray to Him in His agony. I look to the cross. What inspiration does He give?

We will be like St. Paul.

"But because of Christ, I have come to consider all these advantages that I had as disadvantages. Not only that, but I believe nothing can happen that will outweigh the supreme advantage of knowing Christ Jesus my Lord. For him I have accepted the loss of everything, and I look on everthing as so much rubbish if only I can have Christ and be given a place in him. I am no longer trying for perfection by my own efforts, the perfection that comes from the Law, but I want only the perfection that comes through faith in Christ, and is from God and based on faith. All I want is to know Christ and the power of his resurrection and to share his sufferings by reproducing the pattern of his death. That is the way I can hope to take my place in the resurrection of the dead." *(Phil. 3:7-11)*

When we reproduce the pattern of His death, He can help us rise. Most of us want to go from the public life to the resurrection, avoiding the passion. It is so difficult to enter into suffering. We shy away. But, to live in the mystery of Christ's life, suffering, death and resurrection is to live life fully. To believe and have faith does not change the human condition. What it does mean is that we look at the same reality with the eyes of faith, the eyes of Jesus. That can change it completely. As much as He gives the Spirit, life changes.

The sufferings don't disappear, but they take on meaning. The pain does not go away but has a future orientation. It gives hope and the hope is not deceptive because as Paul exclaims to the Romans: "The Holy Spirit has been poured into our hearts." *(Romans 5:5) It is as simple and as deeply profound as that!*

As Christians we claim to follow Christ. There will be moments of laughter, bursts of joy, days of suffering and time of wounding. To be wounded and be with Jesus, or to be wounded and not to be with Him seems to be the alternative. We make the choice. He died that we might accept our death and move on to the resurrection – the miracle and the meaning of Christianity. Life conquers death. Salvation replaces damnation. Our wounded-God-Man heals us. Will our wounds be signs of hope?

His Heart stands so silently still,
> as Judas jangles...confused.
> as Peter peers...bemused.
> as Pilate prods...confusion.
> as soldiers sneer...amusement.
> as we...

His Heart pleads for peaceful presence,
> in lips, thirsting...in eyes, forgiving...
> in eyes, forgiving...
> in side, wounded...
> in hands, reaching...
> in us...

His Heart is 'still-present',
> through broken-bread-consecrated.
> through mixed-wine-transformed.
> through men-women-given.
> through WORD-prayer-shared.
> through us...

Like an eagle landing with a limp,
        life lingers.
A wounded wing and
a tender talon
        talk of time,

                tearing, torn time.
Yet,
        yearnings for circling and soaring and swirling
                surge in the bruised bird.
        memories of dancing on the clouds,
                caressing the currents,
                smiling at the sun
        taunt a tethered spirit.
But,
        mindful of mending,
        hopeful in healing,
        watchful in waiting,

                his heart is still

He waits.

A prayer

Lord You call us to life. We thank You. You invite us to live like You; we struggle. How did You accept Your wounds? How did You accept Your sufferings?...the scourging?...the crowning?...the rejection?...the spitting?...the yelling?...Lord we need Your strength, Your courage. Help us to be wounded-healers. Strengthen us to be like You.

pause...pray...pain.

Jesus before Pilate

So Pilate came outside to them and said, 'What charge do you bring against this man?' They replied, 'If he were not a criminal, we should not be handing him over to you'. Pilate said, 'Take him yourselves, and try him by your own Law'. The Jews answered, 'We are not allowed to put a man to death'. This was to fulfill the words Jesus had spoken indicating the way he was going to die.

So Pilate went back into the Praetorium and called Jesus to him, 'Are you the king of the Jews?' he asked. Jesus replied, 'Do you ask this of your own accord, or have others spoken to you about me?' Pilate answered, 'Am I a Jew? It is your own people and the chief priests who have handed you over to me: what have you done?' Jesus replied, 'Mine is not a kingdom of this world; if my kingdom were of this world, my men would have fought to prevent my being surrendered to the Jews. But my kingdom is not of this kind.' 'So you are a king then?' said Pilate. 'It is you who say it' answered Jesus. 'Yes, I am a king. I was born for this, I came into the world for this: to bear witness to the truth; and all who are on the side of truth listen to my voice.' 'Truth?' said Pilate 'What is that?'; and with that he went out again to the Jews and said, 'I find no case against him.'

Pilate then had Jesus taken away and scourged; and after this, the soldiers twisted some thorns into a crown and put it on his head, and dressed him in a purple robe. They kept coming up to him and saying, 'Hail, king of the Jews!'; and they slapped him in the face.

Pilate came outside again and said to them, 'Look, I am going to bring him out to you to let you see that I find no case'. Jesus then came out wearing the crown of thorns and the purple robe. Pilate said, 'Here is the man'. When they saw him the chief priests and the guards shouted, 'Crucify him!' Crucify him!' Pilate said, 'Take him yourselves and crucify him: I can find no case against him'. 'We have a Law,' the Jews replied 'and according to that Law he ought to die, because he has claimed to be the Son of God.'

When Pilate heard them say this his fears increased. Re-entering the Praetorium, he said to Jesus, 'Where do you come from?' But Jesus made no answer. Pilate then said to him, 'Are you refusing to speak to me? Surely you know I have power to release you and I have power to crucify you?' 'You would have no power over me' replied Jesus 'if it had not been given you from above; that is why the one who handed me over to you has the greater guilt.'

(John 18:29-38; 19:1-11)

The good thief

One of the criminals hanging there abused him. 'Are you not the Christ?' he said. 'Save yourself and us as well.' But the other spoke up and rebuked him. 'Have you no fear of God at all?' he said. 'You got the same sentence as he did, but in our case we deserved it: we are paying for what we did. But this man has done nothing wrong. Jesus,' he said 'remember me when you come into your kingdom.' 'Indeed, I promise you,' he replied 'today you will be with me in paradise.' *(Luke 23:39-43)*

remember. . .recall. . .renew.

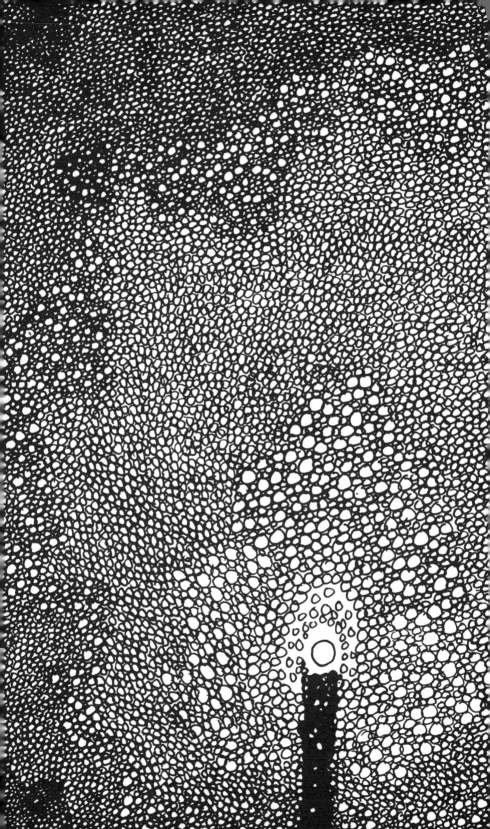

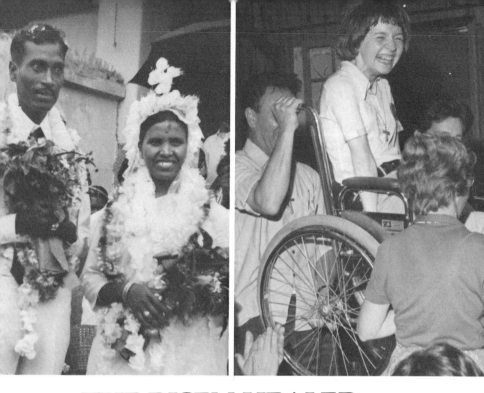

THE RISEN HEALER

Excitement and enthusiasm rippled through the house. Joy and laughter ran wild. It was Kathy's fifth birthday party! Presents, games and birthday cake, topped with chocolate ice cream, bonded their young love. The joy of the celebration kept Kathy wide awake at bed-time. Her heart was still dancing; her eyes were still sparkling.

This deep, human joy reflects the joy of Jesus; often, it is His joy. His resurrection makes all joy possible. He floods our world with His Spirit, the spirit of joy and peace. He wants to dance in our hearts and sparkle in our eyes.

To surge with love for another, to feel joy bubbling up from within, to sigh a breath of deep peace, all touch the spirit of the risen Christ. He infuses the human spirit through His Spirit. He desires love, joy, peace, for all. He is touching minds and hearts, permeating bodies and souls. He longs for change in attitude. He yearns for people of peace. He hopes for hearts of love.

His unique life, His many ways of healing and His friends all bring us to the core of His message. He is the only man in history who rose from the dead. No other man has ever claimed this; nor has anyone ever claimed it for another. Jesus' resurrection authenticates and vitalizes His message. He lives today in His resurrected body. This is the *raison d'être* for our relationship with Him. This is the ground for all meaning of Christian living. All healing ebbs and flows from the Risen Christ.

Jesus is the Lord of the Dance,
     the dance of life, love and laughter!
  He is the Other for others,
    for saints, sots and sinners;
    for aging and anguished
      and all.

Jesus is the spark of joy,
  the smile of love,
  the pulse of peace.
He is the risen healer!

A NEW PRESENCE... to individuals

After His resurrection Jesus encountered Mary of Magdala outside the tomb.

'Woman, why are you weeping?'

'They have taken my Lord away' she replied 'and I don't know where they have put him.'

As she said this she turned round and saw Jesus standing there, though she did not recognize him. Jesus said:

'Woman, why are you weeping.'

'Who are you looking for?'

Supposing him to be the gardener, she said,

'Sir, if you have taken him away, tell me where you have put him, and I will go and remove him.'

Jesus said: 'Mary!'

She knew him then and said to him in Hebrew, 'Rabbuni'– which means Master. Jesus said to her,

'Do not cling to me, because I have not yet ascended to the Father. But go and find the brothers, and tell them: I am ascending to my Father and your Father, to my God and your God.'

So Mary of Magdala went and told the disciples that she had seen the Lord and that he had said these things to her.

(John 20:13-18)

At first Mary did not recognize Jesus. She was sorrowing. She was feeling deep separation from someone she loved. Isn't our experience the same? When we are separated from a loved one – our husband, our mother, a dear friend – we can be caught up in ourselves. The sadness can isolate; the sorrow can pain deeply. The deeper the love, the more the pain.

Recently Michelle, a mentally-handicapped member of Jean Vanier's community in L'Arche, France, visited Canada for the first time. She came to visit friends for her summer vacation. The reunion after a year was tender, deep, and rich. To watch her with Joan revealed deep love. To see her rest and relax recalled previous visits in France. Travel, sightseeing, and picnics punctuated the days of quiet sharing and gentle stillness. But the day for departure came. As the time approached, some tears flowed; sadness came; separation was close. At one point Michelle simply said: "My stomach hurts doesn't yours?" When the actual moment of separation came, she walked over to the car and touched my cheek ever so gently with the back of her fingers saying: "Au revoir, au revoir, père Georges . . ." Needless to say, our eyes glistened; my heart said: 'stay longer,' and desire for another visit welled up. One day . . . somewhere . . . for sure. As I drove quietly down the highway, I mused: 'I sure hope that the joy of our next visit will be in proportion to the pain of this separation.'

For a time Mary of Magdala was caught in her sorrowing. She mistook Jesus for the gardener and asked him if he could help her find His body. She was not locked in totally on herself but was searching and seeking. She was ready to do something. She was open to find Him. "Where have you placed Him?" she pleaded.

When Jesus said: *"Mary!"* she knew Him. She exclaimed: *"My Lord!"* She recognized the Risen Jesus. Was it the timbre of His voice? Was it His intonation? Did His glance take her name to her heart? Did a gesture reveal His resurrection? Whatever the link something happened in Mary. His touch of new life arose within her. The Spirit came. Her faith erupted and love overflowed.

In this moment of truth a new Jesus appears. *"Do not cling to me . . ."* (John 20:17) Jesus does not want Mary to hang on to His personal relationship. A new love is present. He tells her to spread the good news. Give this gift away. Tell all men that Jesus has risen. She becomes a bearer of good news, a woman of hope grounded in a surging love for Jesus and a deep faith in Him. She spreads His message of love. He wants her to speak His word; He desires her to touch tenderly the wounded ones; to bind up the lonely hearts, the estranged minds; He hopes she will love and live like Him. He needs her hands, her heart, her love to present hope to a wounded world, to bring life to a dying planet. Jesus needs Mary in His new economy of loving mankind.

How will we be channels of peace today?
                              tomorrow?
                              and
                              tomorrow?

How will we look with love?
            smile with joy?
            touch with tenderness?

Where will we find hope for the hopeless?
                  faith for the faithless?
                  love for the rejected?
                              jilted?
                              jeered
                              and
                              sneered at person?

        Prostitutes and prisoners pain.
        Doctors and dentists. . .

        Priests and paupers ponder.
        Aging and adolescents. . .

        House wives and handicapped heal.
        Laborers and lawyers. . .

Relate...
Reveal...
Renew...

Trust...
Time...
Tender...

Help...
Heal...
Hope...

Jesus...
Mary...
Me...

In our human experience touches of Jesus' spirit arise. A new infant mellows the hardened heart. A marriage binds families. Anniversaries celebrate fidelity. Birthday parties are fun. Visits with close friends warm the heart. Family reunions can heal hurts and deepen love. Jesus' risen presence through His Spirit pops up everywhere. The gift is to recognize that presence.

The mystery of love unfolds uniquely in these and other interpersonal relationships. We meet someone; something blocks their goodness or our perception. But, a word, a gesture, time reveals their true self and ours too. Friendship begins. Disagreements may happen, but healing comes through honest dialogue. Real acceptance creates mutual trust, growing love and deeper knowledge. True openness invites to a spiralling deep relationship. The ebb and flow of joy and sorrow, laughter and tears, peace and violence spell out an evolving friendship. There is a time to surrender and a time to speak; a time for silent presence and a time for probing discussion; a time for touch and a time for distance; the interpersonal is so deeply a mystery – partly known and partly unknown; sometimes clear and sometimes obscure; moments of peace and moments of confusion; deeply human, surprisingly divine; mixed with hope and despair but ever new, ever future.

This mystery of friendship is like a reverse reality. We think that the more we can amass, the better we will be. We do not really accumulate love. This spiritual force is so unlike material goods. In fact, the more we give it away, the more it seems to increase. It is the same with Jesus. The minute we close in and try to lock up His love, we loose it. If we say to ourselves 'He's mine; I've got Him at last; I'm going to keep Him!' we kill His risen love. In proportion that we desire to give the Lord away, the more He seems to be present. As we share Him, His love and His message, we become more lovingly human. As we encourage people and are present as consolers, healers and friends, the spirit of the risen Lord is there. It almost seems that inasmuch as we want others to have the Lord, He surges and wells up within us. As in each friendship the apparent contradiction is – we grow in love as we give it away. We love with open hands. We do not clasp and cramp people but we hold them with open arms. We free them. We send them forth with an enlivened spirit.

Parents know this truth in their love for their children. From the moment of birth children are potentially free to go. They need total care for some time – feeding, clothing, shelter – but more important the tender hand that caresses their little body with love and the gentle word which speaks lovingly to their open heart and mind. As children grow physically, psychologically and spiritually, they hopefully become more independent and free. Their potential to create, to love and to live expands. They are becoming more human as they prepare to step out and begin their own life journey. The profound relationship with their parents moulds them for life, forms their freedom and calls them to be loving human beings. To watch a father play with his two-year old on the living room floor after supper, to see a mother teach her daughter how to cook coconut cream pie, to know that dad plays golf with his adolescent son or mom crochets with her teenage daughter, all speak of a quality of relationship. This does not come in a day. Love develops with time. Values emerge through sharing, questions, discussions. Bonds build. Life surges. Freedom leads to choice. And one day the young adult forges his own future. Will he create a family, love as a single man or woman, or maybe a priest? Whichever life we live, the call is to love. Our world needs lovers, gentle, tender people, men and women of compassion. People need the presence of the risen Christ, His Spirit, His message of love and peace. How will we incarnate that love?

Jesus told Mary of Magdala to go and tell the brothers about His resurrection. Spread the Good News! The Kingdom has come! With sparkling enthusiasm she shares her risen Lord. This is our hope.

A NEW PRESENCE... to small groups

Luke, one of the first Christians, shares his faith and insight into the personality of the Risen Christ.

> That very same day, two of them were on their way to a village called Emmaus, seven miles from Jerusalem, and they were talking together about all that had happened. Now as they talked this over, Jesus Himself came up and walked by their side; but something prevented them from recognizing him. He said to them,
> 'What matters are you discussing as you walk along?'
> They stopped short, their faces down cast. Then one of them, called Cleopas, answered him,
> 'You must be the only person staying in Jerusalem who does not know the things that have been happening there these last few days.'
> 'What things?' he asked. *(Luke 24:13-18)*

Again Jesus does not reveal Himself immediately. He joins these two travellers as an apparent stranger. Their slow gait and heavy countenances reflect a gloomy mood; their disappointment is evident. When he queries them, they answer. Even with their depression they muster a response to this seemingly total stranger. In some way they are open. They welcome Him to join their little journey.

Sometimes the person we least expect enters our life with a freshness and surprise. One evening on route from Ottawa to Montreal the gas gage was bouncing off empty. With no highway sign to indicate the next service center we turned off to find a gas station on a small side road. After five anxious miles we found a Texaco gas bar open but no unleaded fuel. What would we do? For English speaking people in a small French town this posed a double dilemma. After some hesitation and discussion about using super or reguler in the car the teenage attendant said: *"L'essence sans plomb est a Shell."* He even dialed the telephone number and in broken French, we expressed our need. Another pleasant teenager opened the Shell garage, turned on the pumps and serviced our car. The gentleness and readiness to help touched us; the simplicity and openness to strangers warmed our hearts. We sped off towards Montreal with a full tank of gas and hearts full of hope.

On the way to Emmaus Jesus enters into a dialogue with these men. He playfully pretends that He is ignorant of everything. He asks questions. He walks silently along with them. They describe what has happened.

'All about Jesus of Nazareth' they answered 'who proved he was a great prophet by the things he said and did in the sight of God and of the whole people; and how our chief priests and our leaders handed him over to be sentenced to death, and had him crucified. Our own hope had been that he would be the one to set Israel free. And this is not all: two whole days have gone by since it all happened; and some women from our group have astounded us: they went to the tomb in the early morning, and when they did not find the body, they came back to tell us they had seen a vision of angels who declared he was alive. Some of our friends went to the tomb and found everything exactly as the women had reported, but of him they saw nothing.' *(Luke 24:19-24)*

Jesus listens. Many thoughts and feelings must have run through Him. He must have smiled to Himself for He knew that gradually He would reveal Himself to them. He lets them explain the recent happenings. This is all about Him. What a sense of humor! What playful irony!

The risen Jesus is indeed the playful Christ. His peaceful teasing and gentle leading to the revelation of His resurrection is a deep sign of friendship. Among friends or, even when we first meet someone, playfulness can be a touching sign of affection. To tease with a twinkle in one's eye eases the relationship. The squirt of a water gun, the untying of an apron string or hiding someone's favorite coffee mug can all communicate a playful, easy friendship. People enter each others' lives in simple ways; they encounter each other more deeply as time passes and occasion provides; friendships grow; love expands and hope emerges.

But Cleophas and his friend, maybe Luke himself, are upset. 'Who are you?' 'Don't you understand?' 'Aren't you in the in-group?' 'Aren't you with it?' 'Don't you know what's been happening?' Their wonder and confusion about Jesus is clear. They explain how Jesus was condemned, sentenced and crucified. How did Jesus feel and think when they said this? What moved in His being when they recounted His sufferings? What is the consciousness of the Risen Jesus?

He is that man.

He was handed over, scourged, yelled at . . .

He was spat upon, mocked, jeered at . . .

He was rejected . . .

He died.

He must have thought: 'Look what they observed.' 'This is what they saw and understood.' 'They touched this part of my sufferings.' But Jesus wants to give them more – the fullness of life!

Jesus knew the kind of hope they had. Their hope was for political power. They wanted Him to free their nation from the rule of the Romans. They wanted Him to come in strength and force. They desired control and domination. They wanted to be number one! But this was not the power of Jesus. He knew that He had to touch them with His Spirit. They would eventually become men of invitation and concern, men of gentleness and compassion. Indeed, they would become men who could be wounded but rise one day with Him. With His Spirit they will become men of hope. Then He said to them:

> 'You foolish men! So slow to believe the full message of the prophets! Was it not ordained that the Christ should suffer and so enter into His glory?' Then, starting with Moses and going through all the prophets, He explained to them the passages througout the scriptures that were about Himself.   *(Luke 24:25-27)*

His gentle rebuke challenges their memory of His own teaching and the Old Testament. Perhaps He asked them about the Prophet Isaiah when he said:

> "Because you are precious in my eyes, because you are honored and I love you."   *(Isaiah 43:4a)*

Maybe He asked them to recall Jeremiah's exclaiming:

"Deep within their being I will plant my Law writing it on
their hearts!"   *(Jeremiah 31:36b)*

Or, He may have inquired how often they mulled over Micah's
exhortation:

"This is what Yahweh asks of you: only this, to act justly,
to love tenderly, and to walk humbly with your God."
                                                      (Micah 6:8)

Possibly He may have wanted to know if they had experienced
Ezekiel's prophecy?

"I shall give you a new heart and put a new spirit in you."
                                                      (Ezekiel 36:26)

He goes on questioning and explaining the prophets, pointing from
the Old to the New Testament and opening them up to the full
message. Imagine these two disciples. What was happening in them
as this explanation was unfolding? What were they hearing? Who
was speaking? The Word was speaking the Word. The Word made
flesh was revealing the Word of God. The two are one. There was
only one word that day – Jesus, the incarnate Word. He is the Risen
Word. Then, the human, the beautifully human/divine situation
continues:

When they drew near to the village to which they were
going, he made as if to go on; but they pressed him to stay
with them.

'It is nearly evening' they said 'and the day is almost
over.'
                                                      (Luke 24:28-29)

The disciples are changing. Something is happening. Jesus is making
sense. They want Him to stay with them. They are becoming aware
that He is very special.

So he went in to stay with them. Now while he was with
them at table, he took bread and said the blessing; then
he broke it and handed it to them. And their eyes were
opened and they recognized him; but he vanished from
their sight.
                                                      (Luke 24:30-32)

They recognize Him in the breaking of bread. The flood of His
Spirit come! The flash of faith releases love. They become men
of hope.

Sometimes we recognize Him in the breaking of bread. With the touch of His Spirit the moment of recognition takes many forms. He calls us to be broken like the bread. He invites us to be poured out like the wine. He urges us to sing Alleluia! He inspires us to proclaim that 'Jesus is Lord!' He creates us as men and women of hope. But there are other times when the breaking of bread is quiet, dry and apparently empty. The Spirit does not seem present, except in a deep act of faith. We are prayerfully present saying 'yes' but without the Spirit of Jesus, we are still without the overflow of faith or love. We are helpless creatures when it comes to believing. We experience deep need, real poverty in our human spirit and we hunger and thirst so much. We need His Spirit. But the startling reality remains – we come to the Table of the Lord as we are – weak and poor, faithful or unfree, sinful but hopeful. We present ourselves to the Presence through the Word of Revelation, the breaking of bread and the passing of the cup. What a possibility for healing! What an opportunity to rise!

At the Emmaus meal Jesus vanished at the moment of recognition. He is indeed inviting them into a new relationship. He appears in a unique way but disappears almost immediately, leaving them with a burning desire for more of His message. The spark of His risen love is ignited. His Spirit will fan this flame of faith and fire of peace in their hearts. They will become people of peace.

These friends of Jesus will emerge as the paschal people of His message. Their interior excitement will overflow to exterior celebration. Their joy will flow from their peaceful hearts. Their smiles will come from the inside out, from deep down. Theirs is not a plastic grin but a rippling hope. They will dance with the joy of the Risen Lord. Their life is an integration of living and dying, suffering and rising. Their desire is to incarnate the full message of Jesus – the Risen Healer.

Their very words describe the experience.

"Did not our hearts burn within us as He talked on the road and He explained the Scriptures to us." (Luke 24:32)

New life surged in them. They bubbled with joy. His Spirit filled them. If we have ever experienced our hearts burning in faith, alive with Scripture, dancing with joy, loving to serve, excited about Jesus and His message, we too have His Spirit. We have a faith experience of the Resurrection. We have reason to hope. Love has been poured into our hearts. *(Romans 5:5)* As Teilhard de Chardin said: "When man discovers love, he will discover fire for the second time."

Love motivates people beyond highest expectations. It sends people around the world. It calls people to live in other cultures. It moves people deeply into a commitment. It keeps them faithful. In times of suffering, it supports. In times of separation, it grounds hope. When joy and happiness abound, love intensifies the excitement. When laughter and singing fill the air, love animates the celebration. When dancing and foot-stomping rock the house, people bubble from a loving heart. Indeed, love qualifies life.

The Spirit of the Risen Jesus, this in-dwelling of His love, adds to our personal and social love. The Lord gives richer meaning to celebration; He provides a more solid support through life's vicissitudes; He strengthens us in time of difficulty; His love helps us go beyond ourselves, move out of ourselves. His love touches our love through His Spirit. Our love is linked to His Risen Love. His Spirit touches our spirit. We burn with love – ours and His. We too become disciples, friends of the Lord.

Have you ever met someone whom the Spirit of Jesus has touched? Have you looked into their eyes? listened to their words? watched their actions? felt their love? Often they have an incredible thirst for Scripture and a hunger to know Jesus. Prayer becomes a deep value in their life. Service and love of their friends is essential. They sometimes bend over backwards to help you. Their love often moves them to the needy and rejected. Orphans, prisoners, handicapped – all people become channels of new life. They give and receive; they cry and laugh; they sing and mourn but under it all is a firm hope resting on His Love planted in their hearts by His Spirit. Just like the disciples at Emmaus they have a great desire to spread the good news.

> They set out that instant and returned to Jerusalem. There they found the Eleven assembled together with their companions, who said to them, 'Yes, it is true. The Lord has risen and has appeared to Simon.' Then they told their story of what had happened on the road and how they had recognised him at the breaking of bread.
>
> *(Luke 24:33-35)*

To be still before the Silent Bread,
                    listening/speaking. . .

To be bent as a broken body,
                    waiting/watching. . .

To be given the broken Bread,
                    hoping/healing. . .

To be one of His silent Body,
                    loving/living. . .

A NEW PRESENCE...in community

The Spirit meets us where we are; He comes to the setting of our life. Maybe He has not come the way we expect. We want one thing; He gives another. We desire this, but He gives that; but His presence is with us. We seek our moment of grace. We ask for what we desire. We wait. We hope, and He comes in His time and in His way.

The Risen Jesus is uniquely sensitive to each of us, just as He was to Mary of Magdala and the disciples on the road to Emmaus. Mary wept; she mistook Him for the gardener and mourned His separation. Jesus called her by name. His words touched her heart. Cleophas and his friend are depressed as they plodded homeward. He explained the Scriptures. His words opened their minds.

Imagine what He might have said to us. How He would have called our name? How far would He have walked? How much explanation would He have given? Would He have met us with a sign of affection in word or touch? Or, would He have come through an intellectual encounter? How would He have come? by heart or head, or both?

How does He come today?

A sign of the Risen Jesus often comes in some form of community. He invades the group like He did in the Upper Room.

> In the evening of that same day, the first day of the week, the doors were closed in the room where the disciples were, for fear of the Jews. Jesus came and stood among them. *(John 20:19)*

His followers are frightened. They have locked the doors. Fear pervades the group. He appears.

> "Peace be with you!" and He showed them His hands and His side. *(John 20:20)*

How often fear closes us up, locks us in or walls others out. We isolate ourselves. How will we come out? How will we be freed? How will we grow? Often we will need a community in which to rise from ourselves and live with and for others.

A close friend is alive today but could be among the living dead or the walking wounded. Anne grew up in trying circumstances – no trust, abuse and rejection. She faded from relationships and eventually was hospitalized. Her wounds were emotional. Her pain was so deep that she lost weight and moved in and out of reality. At thirty years old she weighed a mere 75 pounds. Wounded and weak she came to live in a caring community. The beginning was rough, especially for the community. Joan, the woman responsible, had to literally carry her to supper sometimes; other times she might fall down the stairs. Cuts, bruises and crying were part of her life. But the deeper wounds were still the key to healing. Time and tenderness, honesty and love called her to life. A gentle day might end with an honest confrontation. At the right moment someone said: "It's time for you to get me a cup of coffee!" And as happened on that day, Anne brewed the coffee. She moved out of herself in a simple act of love. Joy ran through the heart of Joan and hope sprung up in everyone. A flash of resurrection, a touch of peace, a possibility of loving, of healing, all rumbled in their minds and hearts. This did not happen in a day or a week, not even in a month but more like two years. Fidelity, caring, consistency and tested love brought Anne back to life. She had grown physically; a loving heart has replaced her whining voice; a desire to serve has replaced her need to be carried to supper; a part-time job points to independence and freedom to create her own future. In fact she works exceptionally well with the physically handicapped. Love floods her face these days. Most recently she bounced off her first airplane trip with bubbling joy and excitement to visit her friends. She has indeed risen. She knows healing but she also carries her wounds with her. Life is new but old memories die slowly. Working for others is good but her days in the psychiatric hospital still haunt her. Love, trust and time are slowly healing Anne. She knows love; she lives in hope. She rises and dies and rises daily. Anne lives love. She is a rising healer.

This healing presence in a community brings us back to the Upper Room. Jesus showed his wounds; gave His peace and breathed new life on them.

     'Peace be with you',
He said to them and showed them his hands and his side.
The disciples were filled with joy when they saw the Lord,
and he said to them again,
     'Peace be with you. As the Father sent me, so am I sending you.'
After saying this he breathed on them and said:
     'Receive the Holy Spirit.'   (John 20:20-22)

The disciples are overflowing with joy like Joan and her caring community. Jesus sends his friends to share this joy. They bubble and ooze with new love. But grace varies; the Spirit blows where He will; love does not always invade the hearts of all in the same way. Thomas was not sure.

Thomas, called the Twin, who was one of the Twelve, was not with them when Jesus came. When the disciples said, 'We have seen the Lord,' he answered,

'Unless I see the holes that the nails made in his hands and can put my finger into the holes they made, and unless I can put my hand into his side, I refuse to believe.'

(John 20:24-25)

His doubts are real, like ours. His skepticism finds a place in many minds. He has many friends in our world. Maybe we know the Thomas-experience. Maybe we know the need for a sign. What do we do? Where do we turn? To whom do we go? The words of Peter may ring in our ears:

"Lord to whom shall we go? You have the words of eternal life!"

(John 6:68)

Or the words of the Good Thief on Calvary:

"Remember me when you come into your kingdom."

(Luke 23:42)

But Jesus does affirm and give the sign. He promises the thief eternal life, affirms His choosing of Peter and shows Thomas His hands and side.

Eight days later the disciples were in the house again and Thomas was with them. The doors were closed, but Jesus came in and stood among them.

'Peace be with you'

he said. Then he spoke to Thomas,

'Put your finger here; look, here are my hands. Give me your hand; put it into my side. Doubt no longer but believe.'

Thomas replied, 'My Lord and my God!'

Jesus said to him:

'You believe because you can see me.

Happy are those who have not seen and yet believe.'

(John 20:26-29)

The Spirit implants in Thomas. He doubts vanish. His faith flowers. He responds to Jesus amidst his brothers, within his community. His friends supported him for the week. They shared life together; they waited for the healing. And Jesus came.

Sometimes this healing within a community flourishes in individuals. The joy of Jesus expands their consciousness and enlivens their hearts. They dance and sing. They pray gratefully. Hasel knows this joy. When she first came to L'Arche-Winnipeg from the Institution she was wearing a pair of tattered, white running shoes. She never had had a pair of real shoes. Soon she was fitted with a special pair of therapeutic shoes designed especially to fit feet that looked just a little different. The day the shoes were ready Hasel took the bus downtown to pick them up. She strutted proudly from the bus – the greatest feet since Charlie Chaplin. She arrived home just in time for supper. In the period of quiet after supper Hasel prayed: "I'd like to thank our Heavenly Father for the beautiful new pair of shoes I got today. These are my very first pair of shoes. Also, I'd like to thank our heavenly Father for the lovely new dance we learned at the Y today. And I think everybody should learn a new dance every day . . ."

Whether it is Thomas' profession of faith or Hasel's prayer of gratitude to the Lord of the Dance, their expressions emerge from a community context. The apostles are cooperating, not competing. Hasel is happy, not hated. Their lives are different. They know the love of their friends. They experience acceptance even with twisted feet or a doubting mind. Their community holds them till the time of healing comes, till the Risen Jesus arrives.

United with the Father, Jesus pours forth His spirit upon all peoples. The prophet Joel predicted this promise:

"After this,
I will pour out my spirit on all mankind.
Your sons and daughters shall prophesy,
your old men shall dream dreams,
and your young men see visions." *(Joel 3:1)*

The early Christians experienced this in-pouring at Pentecost. *(Acts 2)* Their lives changed. Faith, love and courage motivated them. They spread this good news. Communities of believers increased. Today these signs of hope are present in our wounded world. Mother Teresa in Calcutta, and her Sisters throughout the world, serve the poorest of the poor. Her home for the dying in Calcutta provides a place of refuge where men and women can die with dignity, knowing someone cares. Jean Vanier and his friends have rescued many mentally handicapped men and women from institutions. L'Arche homes in Haiti and Honduras, in Bangalore and Bouake create hope and give life to a forgotten world. Mixed communities of young and old, married and single, more or less mentally gifted, place their lives in common. These havens of hope dot the globe. Foster homes for delinquent boys and girls provide another option for love. Sister Carm calls her "seven-sons" to new life as they grow through adolescence. Half-way houses for ex-cons and alcoholics are springing up everywhere. Many ordinary folk are also seeking a new form of living. The communes of the late 60's seem to have come and gone but some people are still living a shared life. In Toronto, Canada some 50 or 60 small communities have formed a network for support in this alternate life style. People are seeing a need to share their lives, extend their family circle or live with people who have common interest and goals. The phenomenon of shared life is growing. For the contemporary Christian Jesus' message – "Where two or three gather in my name, I am with you" *(Matthew 18:20)* rings a note of hope. His Spirit brings strength and peace; His presence sustains in times of struggle and strain; He heals and helps. After His resurrection Jesus appeared to many but the truth and emphasis rests in community. Often His disciples and friends were together when the Risen Jesus came. Often He exhorted the group. He sent them out to spread the good news to everyone.

"Lord, grant us your risen spirit. Heal our fear to enter the mystery of others. Grant us courage. Be near with Your Spirit. We need You. Call us to be joyful in good times and in bad, not with a phony joy but in a paschal way. Grant us Your joy, that comes from Your Resurrection, Your death, Your sufferings. Create us as people of joy and hope. Make us, indeed, co-sharers in the life of the risen Lord – in Yourself."

"Go, therefore, make disciples of all nations."   *(Matthew 28:19)*

Just like the early Christians, just like the outstanding Christians of our day we have choices to make...

Will we love?
      pain?
        laugh?
          suffer?

                and live with His people or not?

Will we dance?
      sing?
        care for?
          play?

                and die/rise like Him or not?

The choice is ours.
The gift is His.
    Love.
    Hope.
    Heal.

(John 21:15-17)
'Do you love me more than these others do?'

'Yes Lord, you know I love you.'

'Feed my lambs.'

'Do you love me?'

'Yes Lord, you know I love you.'

'Look after my sheep.'

'Do you love me?'